S0-AHM-979

I am Living to Tell

Surviving incurable cancer without killing my mother, my granny or my ex

Laurie J Beck

Dedication

Thank you, God! If I didn't believe that there was a plan for me, I would not be here. I am thankful every day, knowing that God is right by my side.

My biggest supporter and ongoing inspiration is my husband, Bob. I have such respect for him. I watch him every day, working so hard at his life and mine too. He not only wants to be the best, but wants that for me as well. I am thankful for him hanging in there with me—knowing it was going to be a roller-coaster ride—and allowing me to make choices I felt right for me, no matter the outcome. He encouraged and cajoled me to live forward and has made my dreams come true.

Copyright © 2012 Laurie J Beck

All rights reserved.

ISBN-10: 1475269013

EAN-13: 9781475269017

Contents

Introduction   vii

1 Awaken   1

2 Courage   11

3 Intuition   25

4 Tenacity   43

5 Find Serenity   59

6 Forgiveness   79

7 Positivity (With Intention And A Great
    Big Helping Of Humor)   97

8 Create Energy   125

Acknowledgments   159

About The Author   161

Recommended Reading   163

For more information, visit www.lauriebeck.com.

ORIGINAL BLOOD WORK

2906 Julia Drive
Valdosta, GA 31602
Phone (229) 244-4468
Director: Jackson L. Gates, M.D.

FINAL REPORT

PHONE:
SEX: F
FASTING: NO
ROOM #:
MED REC #:
PATIENT ID:

Patient Notes	Specimen Information
FAX 850-534-4174	ACCESSION #: A5766415 REQUISITION #: COLLECTED: 03/22/2006-2:00PM RECEIVED: 03/23/2006-5:09PM REPORTED: 03/24/2006-4:19AM

Test Name	Within Range	Outside Range	Normal Range	Units
CBC				
WBC		70.80 (CH)	.49-11.69	THOU/CUMM
WBC CHECKED				
RBC		4.05 (L)	4.11-5.13	MILL/CUMM
HEMOGLOBIN		10.4 (L)	11.7-15.5	GMS
HEMATOCRIT		32.1 (L)	35.6-44.9	%
MCV		79.4 (L)	80.6-93.6	FL
MCH		25.8 (L)	26.7-32.3	PG
MCHC		32.5 (L)	32.6-36.0	G/DL
RDW		18.8 (H)	12.0-13.8	%
PLATELET COUNT	213		159-373	THOU/CUMM
NEUTROPHILS		2.5 (L)	44.8-74.2	%
LYMPHOCYTES		95.4 (H)	16.8-44.2	%
FEW SMUDGE CELLS				
MONOCYTES		1.6 (L)	2.0-13.0	%
EOSINOPHILS	0.5		0-5.1	%
BASOPHILS	0.0		0-1.2	%
SED RATE (WESTERGREN)		29 (H)	0-20	MM/HR
TSH	3.38		0.27-4.2	uIU/ML
COMPREHENSIVE METABOLIC PANEL				
CALCIUM	9.6		8.5-10.8	MG/DL
GLUCOSE	93		70-110	MG/DL
BUN	23		6-24	MG/DL
CREATININE	0.9		0.6-1.5	MG/DL
PROTEIN, TOTAL	7.1		6.4-8.3	GM/DL
ALBUMIN	4.3		3.4-4.8	GM/DL
BILIRUBIN, TOTAL	0.3		0-1.0	MG/DL
PHOSPHATASE, ALK.	75		35-104	UNITS/L
AST (SGOT)	27		0-37	UNITS/L
ALT (SGPT)	1		0-40	UNITS/L
SODIUM	140		135-148	MEQ/L
POTASSIUM	3.7		3.5-5.3	MEQ/L
CARBON DIOXIDE	27		22-30	MEQ/L
Note: CO2 values may be decreased by exposure to room air.				
CHLORIDE	102		96-110	MEQ/L
GLOMERULAR FILTRATION RATE (CALC)				
GFR, BLACK	88		>60	
GFR, NON-BLACK	73		>60	

*** Glomerular Filtration Rate is calculated using the MDRD
equation as recommended by the National Kidney Foundation.
The GFR calculation is a no-charge service.

*** FINAL REPORT ***

EXCEPT WHERE NOTED: TEST PERFORMED AT DOCTORS LABORATORY INC., VALDOSTA, GA

| ACCESSION #: A5766415 | MED REC #: | AGE, DOB: 42, 05/11/1963 | BECK, LAURIE | PAGE 1 of 1 |
| PRINTED BY: Administrator 03/27/2006 02:07 PM | | | | |

Introduction:

Stop and Listen

I guess you never really know how you're going to feel when you get news like mine. I was only forty-two when I started feeling tired. I felt a bone weary so-knocked-out-tired I couldn't do anything. That wasn't right. I keep myself in great physical condition.

When I finally got the courage to go to an internist, I got the news. It was worse than I could ever imagine.

I now realize that the day I found out I not only had a marginal case of leukemia, but an incurable form of lymphoma was the beginning of the first day of my new life. The cancer I contracted was considered especially rare for someone my age. I was told there was no cure for what I had.

I was stunned into a mental paralysis.

I am not a "drama queen." We've been told over and over that we should make "this day" the "best day" of our lives? How do you make the day you found out that you were going to die be the "best day" of your life? Is that even remotely possible? How does life ever prepare you to think about dying?

I have spent a lifetime taking care of myself. I eat well, exercise, and own a Pilates studio to help other women get into shape. I also had no idea how badly "poisoned" my body was and even worse, how much emotional baggage I was carrying around with me all the time.

It's now four years later, and I have had numerous tests which indicate that I no longer have any cancer at all — none, zilch, zippo — anywhere invading my body. They do say that the cancer is latent and could return. Basically, I am still living with an incurable cancer, but the tests don't register the disease.

It doesn't really matter if I'm not completely "cured". When I got the first test back that showed normal blood counts and no cancer markers, I let out a whoop that could shatter glass. I went from having a death sentence to having the most beautiful, amazing gift God, fate, the Universe, call it what you will, can ever receive, a second chance at life! I am a living affirmation. My daily mantra is "I am healthy and free!" I am strong, in shape, and helping others". That is something I say and believe at least once a day, every day.

My doctors tell me, that I am a "one percenter," meaning that about 1 percent of all people with this form of cancer go into spontaneous remission without some form of medicine(chemo). I am what they call an anomaly.

Healing is a journey. If it were not for a couple of really for-tuitous events, I don't know if this journey would have such a happy ending. I have a wonderful doctor that adopted a "watchful-waiting" stance with the disease raging through my body. And I have a mother who believes in acupuncture and a big dose of humor.

But when I say "fortuitous," I know I had someone watching out for me. I had signed up for chemo and was one day away from having a port inserted. I wasn't sure about that route — how encouraged can anyone be if you're told that putting these really nasty poisons into your body would rid you of the cancer. And there is no ultimate cure? If this cancer usually comes back after treatment, then why would I do it? It was a question that caused all sorts of emotional drama in my house. My loving, wonderful, and very opinionated husband — was convinced that I must start treatment immediately. He's the one who booked all the appoint-ments. In his defense, he was scared to death because his mother had just been diagnosed with terminal brain cancer. He was fran-tically trying to hold on to me in the only way he knew — through the tenets of modern Western medicine — and who can blame him?

For now, God graces me with new life. And I feel led to share some of my healing medicine and give you the eight little lessons of hope I discovered through my healing process. I want to share my path to survival. Whether it is you finding out you have something devastating or knowing a loved one, friend, or acquaintance is in the fight for their life, I hope that my story will encourage you and nurture you on your journey, whatever that journey may be.

What follows is a story about faith, forgiveness, listening, and loving. It is about letting go of deep resentment and abandonment, about releasing old messages so that you can follow your true path and life's purpose. It is proof there are miracles, for I was delivered from a life-threatening disease.

But what's most important is simple — I hope that my story will inspire you to listen to your inner voice, to let go, and to learn to truly love yourself so that you can *live!*

Awaken

CHAPTER 1

First Signs

Stop and listen. This is something most of us are not very good at, and that included me when I first began my journey. When I tell you something was gnawing at me daily, maybe even hourly, I'm not exaggerating. There was a message being delivered to me, and it was now my choice to listen. I decided to go to a doctor after discovering some odd things occurring in my body. I thought I was just going to the doctor because, maybe, I had a sleep disorder or some kind of mono. I was fatigued all the time, and no matter what I did, I couldn't find a way to make myself feel better. I never in my wildest nightmares thought I would hear what I heard.

But my inner voice was strong, and the message was loud: I needed to stop and listen to what my body was telling me, or I wasn't going to be that fun-loving, young Mimi (that's my favorite term for *grandma*) I always wanted to be. There was a problem, though. Stopping and listening was not something I was good at doing. Like most people, I loved to hear myself talk, but that's very different from listening.

I also was inflicted with a common American disease: I had to be chronically busy. My personality — or disease — was to keep going, stay busy, be productive. I based my worthiness on how busy I was. I didn't feel right unless I was doing something. I felt the only way to be productive was to be busy and never to have enough time to sit and think.

When I was a little girl of about ten, I would visit with my grandmother for the summer. All my friends talked about having fun during the summer. Ha! Not with Grannie. If we tried to sleep in late, she would purposely bang pans in the kitchen so we would wake up. Or if the phone rang, she talked loud enough so we could hear. Once we were out of bed, my brother and I were busy little soldiers.

Grannie decided we should take swim lessons so that we would be expert swimmers; she had a small bungalow at the beach in the Hamptons. Swim lessons just happened to be at seven every morning, rain or shine. Do you know how cold Long Island Sound is at seven? An ice chest is warmer. I was not just a hard worker; I wanted to please Grannie and be a good swimmer. So I passed all my tests and got to advance to the next level. It was a curse. The better you got, the longer you stayed in the water. No rest for the chilled.

After swim lessons, it was off to the library for summer reading. When we got home, we would have chores and lunch, and then finally we could go to the beach to play. By the time I got to the beach, I was exhausted and ready for a nap. But there was no napping on Grannie time. There was no "vacation" at Grannie's. She had us hopping, jumping, and fetching. I guess I ended up carrying this philosophy of doing into my lifestyle. It became my way of life. I would feel guilty if I actually sat down. I never learned how to be still and listen.

Boy, has all that changed.

Begin at the Beginning

Listening is an art. I didn't understand what that meant — until now. I would partially listen or think I was listening. But I was hearing only what I wanted to. Or as the old saying goes, "In one ear and out the other." I was excellent at the latter. So I wasn't listening to my body, though it was giving me some pretty loud indications something was incredibly wrong.

It began with an odd rash that kept appearing just under and on the side of my right breast. I kept thinking, *This is odd*, but then would think, *Not really*. I teach a lot of Pilates and tend to sweat under my arms, so I figured the rash was a reaction to my sweat. And I got creative in my "fixes." I would constantly change my shirt, put cotton pads under my armpits close to the rash, or slather on specialty powders, ointments, or gels. I tried it all. The rash would go away and then return. Something gnawing at me kept saying, "This is odd." It was almost like I was hearing voices, but of course I wasn't listening. I didn't want to face up to any hard truth, so I brushed it off.

This went on for about three months. I showed the rash to everybody, including my clients. I asked them, "Have you ever had a rash like this?" and asked for suggestions. Then the rash began to spread after I took a shower. A different rash would suddenly pop up and quickly spread across my bottom and lower back. I didn't pay any attention. I simply justified this with "Maybe the shower was too hot." It didn't matter that the rash would appear no matter what the water temperature was.

This went on for another three months. It was becoming an annoying pattern. Something would start happening with my body, and I would look for something to try to explain it away: I must be allergic to my detergent or my deodorant or my lotion, or I must be sweating a lot, or the heat is finally getting to me.

I finally gave in and went to the doctor. The first doctor said it was something-something dermatitis. Well, that seemed reasonable to me, and off I went with several pricey lotions and potions. But it was the same scenario; I would put on some lotion or gel, and the rash would go away for a day or for just a few hours. I did this for a couple of months, and since nothing was getting better, I decided to get another opinion.

Another dermatologist said, "Oh, we see this all the time." At this point, the rash had spread and covered most of my torso. I walked away with another extremely expensive prescription and started the process all over again. The lotions worked for a bit, and then the rash would reappear. I would get a different lotion. And the rash would come back. It was driving me more than a little crazy.

Intuition

Call it what you will, but never in my life have I had such a strong sense that I should examine my body — I mean, thoroughly examine it. I finally decided to start paying attention, to listen to that inside voice. I was in the shower and decided it would be a good time to do a breast exam. I did them regularly, but they would usually consist of feeling the girls up and around. I would send them some love and be done. This exam was a little more intense. I decided to take my thumbs and dig them straight up into my armpits. *Hmmm.* I felt a lump deep in my upper left armpit. I decided to do the same on the right side. *Oh good*, I thought, *same large lump in the same place. This is a good sign. They must belong there.* I was that unwilling to look at the possibility that something was wrong.

But, being the person I am, I decide to start asking my female clients, "Is it normal to have large lumps deep up in our armpits?"

One gal, who is a doctor's wife, said, "Well, that's where your lymph nodes are." I love it when I learn something new. I never knew my lymph nodes were there.

She seemed knowledgeable, so I asked, "Are you supposed to be able to feel them?"

"Well, no, not really."

I think, *Oh great, I can really feel them.* I decided not to ask any more questions, because I was starting to scare myself. But I couldn't let it go. I started to dig my thumbs under my armpits about ten times a day, making my armpits sore. I felt the lumps each time. *Well*, I thought, *if I didn't have something wrong before, I certainly have created something now. It serves me right.*

I should explain something about myself. I am somewhat of a hypochondriac. My husband, Bob, knows this and teases me constantly. I've never let anyone else in on my little secret. Ever since I was a child, if anyone had something wrong, I would think, *I'm definitely getting it.* I could actually create the sensation in my body; it was almost scary. As I got older, I was neurotic about it. If someone had a disease or a simple cold, I would go home and do my research to make sure I didn't have the symptoms. Now, top that one.

The good news is I'm not crazy about doctors. So while I was finding all sorts of "illnesses" in my body, I was not continually going to the doctors. I would take on the disease for a while and then finally let it go. I think this started when I went to visit my dad's mom, Nana. She had multiple sclerosis, and I felt so sad around her. She could move very little, so she was mostly bedridden. She couldn't do anything for herself. Nana's disease frightened me. The message I heard from who knows where was "Someday one of you will probably get this disease, because it's hereditary." But I didn't want to buy into that, so I did my research. Multiple sclerosis usually appears sometime in a person's thirties or early forties. I was fast leaving the early forties part of my life, so I thought, *I'm in the clear. That's not the chosen disease for me.*

I'm not a big pill popper. Maybe that's partly what has saved my life — at least up to this point. Don't get me wrong; if I have a headache, I will go for the occasional ibuprofen. I don't buy into the mindset that I need to fix things immediately with a pill. I've always been wary of pills, because they have so many side effects — listen to the commercials for something as simple as an antacid pill. Something definitely is not right if you get more problems from taking a pill than what it's supposed to cure in the first place. I'm also enough of a worrier that I don't want to put something into my body when no one, including the FDA, is sure of the long-term effects. While I do believe this habit of taking on others' illnesses played a large role in my condition, my distrust of the easy fix was in large part what saved me.

One morning, in the middle of my constantly feeling up my armpit, I turned my head in the mirror to check for bed head. I have fairly short hair, and I'm a no-fuss kind of girl. I like to be ready to go in twenty minutes. I run a brush through my hair, and I'm done. On this morning, I felt compelled to turn my head and look with a second mirror to see the back of my head. Instead of seeing my hair, I was staring at three lumps traveling down my neck. Again that *hmmm* feeling arose in me.

I brushed it off as scar tissue from a childhood accident. Then I asked all of my clients to look at my neck, and sure enough, each one had something different to share. So, let's see, it's been six months since I first discovered the rash. It's now spreading, with lumps in my armpits and down my neck. I had formulated good reasons for all of them. And I refused to listen to the most important entity in the whole process — my body. I ignored all of the warning signs and went on merrily with life — for a little while longer, that is.

Wine and Spleen

I do believe that my love for wine also helped save my life, or at least extend it. I had decided to open a bottle of wine — something I do on a regular basis. Well, the cork wasn't coming out as easily as usual, so I decided to prop it against my belly and pull. When I did this, I felt an odd soreness in my abs. Actually, it was right underneath my left rib cage. My mind said, *Wow, you must have really worked those abs out yesterday.* My justification made perfect sense. I'm a Pilates girl, and it's all about the abs. I let that "ouch" feeling go. A couple of days later in my studio, while lying on a box teaching, I felt pressure under my left rib cage again. It was like I couldn't get comfortable. This went on for several weeks.

One day, I was leaning against my kitchen counter, and that area still felt tender. Every day I work my abs, but I had never felt this feeling. I did make a "note to self," but I only added it to my growing list: rash, lumps, sore under left rib cage. Do you think it's time to go back to the doctor? Nah, let me give it a little longer.

Tired All the Time

What finally made me break down and go to an internist? My husband, my nagging husband. I have a Pilates studio at the beach. Life is good. I love what I do, and I love to teach—sometimes too much. My schedule is ideal. I teach from eight to one, come home, rest a little, and then work on other things. Well, my new schedule at that point was definitely different. I would still go to the studio, teach, and come home, but then I'd nap for the afternoon and be exhausted the rest of the day. This was definitely not making Bob very happy. He made comments like "Why are you working? This is not benefiting me or you. You're tired all the time."

Of course, I had an answer to these comments. At first I chose to ignore what he was saying. I convinced myself he was jealous of what I was doing. I couldn't have been happier. My star was finally shining, and for the first time in my life, I felt some independence. I liked teaching, coming home, resting, and not waiting on everybody else. One of my boys was in college; the other was in high school. I figured it was my time to be waited on, and I was going to enjoy every minute of it.

This plan was not working. In fact, it was creating a lot of tension and resentment between my honey and me. I continued to ignore my exhaustion, until one day I walked up three flights of stairs. *Wow, am I getting old or what?! I'm totally out of breath.* I was only forty two at the time. *I'm not old, and I teach breathing. This makes no sense.*

Question to Bob now, not my clients: "Honey, do you get out of breath walking up the stairs?"

"Sometimes, yeah."

"Okay, good, then it's not just me."

Stop and Listen

Stop and listen—this is one of the most profound lessons I've learned in my life. I was so busy *doing* that I never allowed what needed to come into my life to enter. I made decisions based on emotions or on "what will be, will be." Most of the time, I never gave it much thought. If something was wrong, I never asked for help. I just got quiet—but I still wasn't listening. I just withdrew, trying not to make waves. This is not a recipe for healthy living— I am living proof of that.

A lot of messages were delivered to me, but I missed about 90 percent of them. I'm not just talking about the warning signs of cancer here. Not listening to myself was epidemic in my life, and it finally took "incurable" cancer to happen before I actually understood. But when I did stop and listen, I heard. A message was being delivered to me loud and clear this time. The message was "Stop what you're doing; it's time to make changes."

There I was, finally living my dream life in a good place. Many life struggles were behind me, or so I thought. I was living a healthy, clean, fulfilled life. *Why me?* I asked. *Why now?* I knew, deep down, that something was wrong, but I still didn't want to listen. And the most ironic thing is, I should have been listening to what *I* was saying—literally.

When I say I was living a healthy lifestyle, I need to clarify that a bit. It's wasn't completely healthy. I was extremely fanatical about trying to live a healthy lifestyle. I ate well, but I never enjoyed what I ate; I ate it because it was good for me. I exercised, but to the point of excess. I wanted everything in my life to be perfect, and I was obsessed. And the kicker? I would always joke with my friends, "Yeah, I eat right, exercise, don't smoke, laugh, have a loving husband—all the good things—but someday I will end up with something good, you watch."

Wow, what does that mean? You may be saying, "So, Laurie, you materialized that cancer into your body." And you are absolutely correct. But I couldn't see that at the time. All I knew was that several of my friends drank like fiends, smoked, and were overweight and unhappy. Oh, and they are all older.

But they didn't have rashes or lumps everywhere. They didn't get winded like I did—even the ones that smoked—and they had energy. I was so damn tired by noon that I couldn't even tie my shoes. I fought it to the last thought. I kept telling myself, *Here I eat as pure as possible, exercise every day, love my life, love what I do, and have finally achieved a balanced lifestyle. There can't be anything wrong with me.*

There's a definite difference between lying to yourself and actually listening to what your body is telling you.

At one point, I *finally* got it. My nagging husband, the rashes, the lumps. Something told me to go to the doctor.

Courage

CHAPTER 2

You Want Me to Do What?

I don't know about you, but I hate going to the doctor. Pretty much everyone I know hates to go to the doctor. I don't like it because it makes me feel powerless. I can't recall going to any doctor and feeling like I had a real answer about what might be going on in my body. Most doctors seem to have the attitude that it's a privilege to be in their presence, that I am more of an experiment to them than a person. The thing I wondered was, if they are all-knowing gods in white coats, why do they always say, "It could be this, but we need to do more tests to determine the problem," or "Let's try that and see what happens." But even after a battery of tests, there was still no definitive answer.

But this time, I wasn't so adversarial. I needed to find the answer. Things were a little different; I knew something was wrong. I was feeling worse every day. That was enough of a scary feeling, so I decided to suck it up. I would cooperate, no matter what kind of doctor I saw.

The First Exam

Some doctors just aren't that exciting and personable. That's okay. Others may be very good practitioners, but they don't know how to make a patient feel comfortable, let alone feel at ease. The doctor I got was my worst nightmare.

Here is what I remember about going to Dr. Personality — the nickname I secretly gave my internist. He had absolutely no bedside manner. Maybe I brought it on myself, because I didn't have a warm and fuzzy feeling going into his office. While I know that's my problem, I definitely had a put-out feeling when he asked, abruptly, "Why are you here?"

Forcing myself not to say anything nasty, I took a Pilates breath to calm my nerves and rattled off my list. I basically got no response. No questions. Not even a change in facial expression. On go the rubber gloves, and the process begins.

Why does he need to put on rubber gloves to touch my lumps? I wondered. While there are medical reasons, good ones, it didn't give me an ounce of comfort. Couldn't he have at least said, "I do this with all my patients," so that I wouldn't feel like I had something infectious *and* deadly?

As he poked and prodded, I told him about the lumps under my arms and neck. He checked those areas but still didn't say anything.

He told me to lie down and checked my spleen. "Wow," he said, "it's quite enlarged."

My God, he can talk! But I wasn't in the mood to have a nice conversation at this point, so I simply grunted, "Yeah, so what does that mean?"

"Well, I'm not sure. The lumps are not a good sign either." That's all he said.

Oh great, I thought. Then Dr. Personality said, "Come back tomorrow. We need to do some blood work."

At that point, I'd had enough. I said, not too kindly, "That's silly. I'm here now. Let's get it done." It made sense to me. I was there, and who did he think he was? I picked him out of the phone book because he was close to home. I also thought I should see an internist, because the dermatologists hadn't helped. I'd figured out that what was wrong with me was an inside deal. I thought I either had a thyroid imbalance or mononucleosis. I was also being cynical; I figured he wanted me to come back the next day so he could charge me for another office visit.

Fortunately, he didn't fight me, but he wasn't nice about it either. He took my blood, none too gently, and said he would call me in a couple of days with the results. I wasn't feeling too hot when I entered the building, but by then I was really feeling like crap. The worst part of the whole visit was that I left knowing nothing. I knew I had an enlarged spleen, but why?

The next three days were hell, seventy-two or so hours of crazy thoughts. I spent more time asking my clients questions than actually helping them with their Pilates. I was finding it very hard to focus. I didn't know what to expect. I wanted to downplay the whole thing, because my mother- in- law was already going through radiation for lung cancer. My darling husband was Mom's caretaker day in and day out. I could tell this was taking a toll on him. I didn't want to add to his stress.

The Phone Call

For three very long days I taught in my studio. I tried to concentrate, but crazy thoughts kept entering my mind. My husband, sensing my worry, said things like, "Honey, you're perfectly fine. You're solid as a rock." I wanted to believe him.

Finally, the phone rang and Dr. Personality's number showed on the caller ID at my studio. I took a deep breath. "Hello?"

"Ms. Beck."

"Yes."

"I have your test results."

"Okay, give them to me."

"Well, the results are not good."

"What does that mean?"

"Your white blood count is eighty thousand."

"Sooooo?"

"Well, normal range is between four thousand and nine thousand."

"Soooooooo?"

"This seems potentially like some form of leukemia."

"I don't understand. I thought only children get that sort of thing."

He let me know that he had a call in to a specialist, an oncologist.

"What's that?" I was feeling impatient and scared. I really didn't know what he was telling me.

"It's a cancer doctor."

Now, at that very moment, I felt some kind of heavy cosmic shift within my space. I felt as though my body had been invaded by aliens. My mind was listening, but as he was telling me this news, I was numb. It's as though I were in some kind of sick movie. Literally, I felt as if I had spun around, and the Laurie I knew was gone forever. I was all of a sudden swept up by the Starship Cancer aliens, never to return.

Truth is, I can't explain how I felt at that moment. Once I was told that I had something serious, even if I didn't know what "it" was, I felt different. I was different. It was a defining moment, realizing that I wasn't going to live forever. This was real. My days might be numbered.

I was forever changed. Just how I was changed would be revealed to me in bits and pieces. This was one journey I wasn't ready to pack my bags for.

I hung up the phone, wishing I had taken the call at home rather than at the studio. My clients were waiting for me to speak — the women who had endured my many questions about *why*. "I just got the news from my doctor," I said, adding that I could have some form of leukemia but needed further testing. I let them know I was leaving immediately, and the studio would be closed for the rest of the day. I don't remember what they said. I just closed up shop and got in my car. Nothing even looked the same as I drove out of the parking lot as I had thousands of times.

Welcome to the Wonderful World of Cancer

My ride home took an eternity, even though my house was three minutes away from the studio. In those three minutes, I had to decide what to do. *Who do I tell? And how do I tell the people news like this?*

It was all made worse by the fact that Bob had called me a few hours earlier in the day to tell me his mother, who had completed thirty-seven treatments of radiation for lung cancer, had now been diagnosed with inoperable brain cancer. She smoked for fifty years; the lung cancer was going to take her eventually, but it was certainly not easy for Bob to hear.

But I had to tell Bob, no matter what. But who else? My dad? We weren't on the best of terms, but yes, he should know. Mom? Mom and I had hardly spoken for the past three years because of something Grannie had done. And all I could do was ask myself, *Do I want to bother her?* The last few times I had talked to her were very uncomfortable. Then I thought of my boys. My boys! How could I even begin to have that conversation with them? That made me start to cry.

I pulled into the garage, wiped my eyes, and decided not to be dramatic about it. Cancer is curable, after all. I walked into the house and gave my honey a kiss. He was already upset about his mom, so I just said, "I got my test back too."

"Yeah?"

"I have leukemia."

"What? What's that?" He was as clueless as I was about it, and he certainly didn't know how serious it was.

"It's some kind of cancer."

"Are you kidding?" It's almost like he didn't want to believe me. He held me and said everything will be okay.

I looked at him again and said, "I've been told I might have cancer." Again he looks at me in disbelief. I swear he looked at me just like I would look at my boys when they were acting up. I could almost hear his thoughts: *I know you just want some extra attention, because I've been so focused on my mom.* But what could he say? We fell into somber silence.

The next person to call was my dad. He didn't say much, because what could he say to such news? I, on the other hand, had lost all my resolve not to be dramatic and was crying on the other end of the phone. I don't remember what he said to me. I just remember hanging up and staring at the phone for a couple of seconds. I took another calming breath and dialed my mom's number.

It was hard to punch out those eleven numbers. Mom and I hadn't been on the best of terms for most of my life. I had so much anger and resentment built up toward her, I remember thinking she didn't deserve the call. I was still holding onto years of childhood resentment and abandonment. But I forced myself to dial.

Phone rings.

She answers. This is rare. Mom is a motivational speaker and is always traveling and unavailable.

"Hi, Mom."

Long silence on the other end.

I blurt out, "Well, I just got some interesting news from the doctor. I was told I might have cancer and that I need to go to an oncologist for further testing. So, what do you think of that?"

Maybe, it's an older generational thing, but she didn't say anything for what seemed like an eternity. What she did say — or rather what I remember her saying — was something that sounded ludicrous to me at the time: "I want you to go get a massage or maybe some acupuncture."

A massage? Acupuncture? Was she nuts? I knew nothing about the therapeutic benefits of either of those. All I could think was, *Boy, I already don't like you, Mom, but this adds fuel to the fire.* But I didn't say that. Instead, I gave her the benefit of the doubt. It couldn't be easy hearing your daughter has cancer.

I repeated, a little more emphatically, "Did you hear what I just said?"

I don't remember exactly what she said, but I do remember that she ended the conversation with "Yes, and go get some acupuncture."

Typical response from Mom, I think. *She doesn't care. All she wants is to go back to her busy, selfish life.*

I then shared Mom's interesting advice to my husband. He disliked my mom more than I did, so this only inflamed his dislike toward her. He started spouting a tirade against her, but I didn't want this to be about my mom, so I told him that wasn't going to help. I don't remember what we talked about, but I do remember feeling numb and then getting angry. I didn't know what to think at that point. I just wanted it to all go away. But the lumps, the rashes — they all told me otherwise. Most of all, I was scared.

The Oncologist

Dr. Personality called and said that my appointment with the oncologist was in two weeks. I wasn't feeling good about Dr. P.'s recommendation, so I thanked him and called a friend who had been an oncology nurse. Ginny got me an appointment, also two weeks away.

Those two weeks were extreme torture. I had never been so overwhelmed in my life. I didn't eat. Ginny was so supportive, but I knew she knew something just by reading my blood work. I could sense it wasn't good, but I didn't press her for information. I didn't want more bad news.

Ginny told me that the best thing I could do at that point was to get informed. She brought me some medical books and told me about some websites to explore. Bad idea; I spent hours on the computer, sometimes even waking up at 2:00 a.m. and surfing the Net, terrorizing myself. By the time I was done with all my research, I decided there was no need to go on. Worst-case scenario, I had six months; best, two years. I never knew there were so many subcategories of one disease.

Finally it was time to make the four-hour drive. Ginny had been a nurse at this particular hospital and had amazing connections. She got me an appointment with the head doctor of oncology. Lucky me.

On the trip there, Bob and I barely spoke. Nothing seemed real. I was in the middle of a bad dream, and I couldn't wake up, though that was what I desperately wanted to do. I remember thinking, *Why even bother?* The Internet information had practically condemned me to death. Furthermore, all my research convinced me there was one test I would refuse, a painful bone biopsy. I kept telling myself, *I'll do blood work, anything, but I'm not doing that.*

Blood Tests

When we entered the hospital building, I felt like I had stepped into another world. I had gone from working with healthy people, training them in Pilates so that they could be strong, to my own very crazy, sick world. When I walked into the oncology clinic, I couldn't imagine that so many ill people existed. I'm not talking twenty to thirty people—more like hundreds. I thought, *How is it possible that I'm here? Sure, I'm tired all the time and have all these lumps, but I basically feel fine.* I still wanted to believe that there was nothing wrong with me.

So there I was, in an environment that decided life and death. I read department names that I'd never heard of. What was a hematology suite? Was this some luxury spa, right in the middle of all these sick people? What a nice idea. I knew what *oncology* meant, and I didn't want to think about radiology, but what about *infusion*? The names alone made me feel ill.

Check-in time. *Oh boy, here we go.* In about a minute, I went from having a name to becoming a number. Once I had my number, they sent me over to administration. They needed my insurance papers to make sure I could pay. Bob sent me to process my paperwork, and I was miffed. There I was, feeling confused, even a little angry and frustrated, and he was socializing with my friend. Where was my knight in shining armor when I needed him? It just didn't seem fair that I was going to this party alone.

At that point I was happy I could still sign my name. I filled out the obligatory forms as the chip on my shoulder was growing into a boulder. I met with the doctor and told him what I was experiencing. He checked my spleen. Boy, do I now know where that organ is and all its functions. We talked for a bit, and he read my blood work. He wanted to recheck the blood work in case there was a mistake. I was hoping he would say that. Yes! *Dr. P. must have screwed up. I do not belong here. I have a life, and this is a very big mistake.*

He sent me to the lab for more blood work. I was thinking, *One vial like before, and I'll be outta here.* Boy, was I fooled. They took me to a not-so-nice area full of very sick people. There were ten uncomfortable chairs with people sitting in them, waiting for the technician to call them and draw their blood.

I found out quickly the Hematology Suite was not a spa. They called my number. The lab tech had me sit down. She tied my arm, none too gently, and began taking vial after vial out of my arm. No greeting. No joke. Fifteen vials later, she said, "You're done."

At that point I was ready to pass out. I had barely eaten anything for two weeks, so I was at my weakest point since the whole process began. I asked for some juice so that I wouldn't faint. From her reaction, you'd think I was asking for a gourmet meal that was going to take hours to prepare. I was definitely edgy.

No Rest for the Weary

The doctor reentered the room after my blood work to discuss the results. I continued to hope that my internist was wrong and that I would be on my way home. I'd return to my faux healthy and happy life—faux because I was soon to find out how many aspects of my life were toxic and detrimental to the very health and happiness I craved at that moment.

Boy, was I delusional. The news actually got worse. The doctor proceeded to say, "Not only are we seeing some form of leukemia, but there is some form of lymphoma as well." I asked, "What does that mean. Is this good?"

"Well, we've never quite seen it like this."

I was afraid to ask what he meant by that. What I do remember thinking is, *Great, I haven't studied this disease yet.* I'd heard about it—actually, I knew a young woman who had passed away from it about ten years prior—so I knew lymphoma couldn't be good.

The doctor then said, "The only way we can confirm all that we are seeing from the blood work is by doing a bone marrow biopsy."

Oh crap. This is when my mind actually left my body. My worst fear was realized. I believed that God was playing some sick joke on me. Either that, or I was back in my endless nightmare.

What did I do to deserve this? I went down my list. *I'm a good wife, mother, daughter...*oops, that's where I failed, I know it. My mom always said that if I continued to be angry, something like this would happen. I wasn't about to dive into all the mixed feelings I had about my mother. I had to concentrate on the moment.

Though I had decided before walking into the hospital that I'd refuse this test, I didn't—and I don't know why. He scheduled the test for the next morning. That was convenient, since we were staying overnight at a nearby hotel. When we'd checked in that hotel before going to the hospital, I thought we would go back to the hotel ready to celebrate, drink some wine, and have a wonderful dinner. My plan was not in the playbook.

I looked at the doctor. "You *are* kidding, right?"

"Sorry, I wish I were."

When they say a memory is etched in your mind forever, I'm going to put this one in that category. That moment felt like a lifetime; the next twenty-four hours, an eternity.

Bob was practically speechless at this point. Again, what could he have possibly said that would have made me feel better? We went back to our hotel, and I had mentally left the planet. I thought, *I'm starting to get real good at this*. I decided that if I could make myself disappear right then, that would be even better.

The night before the bone marrow test was the worst. I couldn't eat. I was exhausted but couldn't sleep. I remember finally falling asleep around eleven, but two hours later, I was wide awake. My mind was racing like I was Secretariat at the Kentucky Derby.

I was trying to be positive. *Maybe the bone marrow test will show something good and that all this is a mistake.* But I was too paralyzed to put any oomph into that positive thought. More thoughts volleyed. I wanted to know what could happen if my test came back negative, but then I didn't want to know. *Sometimes knowing too much is not a good thing,* I thought. But then I told myself, *Not exploring your options could be deadly as well.* The voice was annoying.

Wide awake, I looked over at Bob, who was sleeping peacefully. Now I was really pissed. *How dare he sleep while I'm terrorizing myself? I'm the one that has to do this god-awful test.* Then I thought, *Maybe he should have the test too.*

But I knew he needed his sleep. He had driven to the hospital, gone to my appointment, and waited all day. He was supposed to drive us home after my test. I had exhausted myself to a point of insanity and irrationality, and I didn't want him to know I had totally lost it. I also knew he would have said all the right things if I really needed to wake him.

As I began the whole healing journey, I would wake him many times. He would stay up for hours just talking and listening, but not that night.

Making It through the Night

I did have a real problem. We had a room, not a suite. There was nowhere to go. I couldn't turn on a light, because that would wake Bob. After two more hours of tossing and turning, I went into the bathroom. I drew a warm bath, and as I lay in the tub, I thought about all the worst places this disease could take me.

One of the other pieces of advice Mom had given me during the two weeks that I waited for that exam was to get some Xanax. For the first time in a long time, I had listened to her. I decided to take a pill. When I take a pill I always imagine the worst, and I couldn't help but chuckle at the irony. *Why worry? It doesn't get any worse than this.* Then my thoughts turned dark. *Maybe I should just take the whole bottle and be done with it. At least I would get out of taking these scary tests.*

I was truly freaked out about the test. They were going to drill into my iliac crest—the top part of my pelvic bone. How barbaric. They literally bore into the bone area to aspirate marrow out of the bone. *Why can't they just knock me out?* I thought. *Oh, I know why. I don't like to be put to sleep.* At that point, I wasn't sure which was worse, going to sleep and never waking up, or being awake and feeling the pain of my life.

I went back into the room and get pissed all over again. My darling husband was sleeping—so peacefully. Nothing bothers him. We could be in a tornado, and he would tell me, "It's no big deal." Why wasn't he on bone marrow biopsy alert like me? Why wasn't he preparing for this horrible experience?

I lay there in bed for another two hours, going over my whole life. *Why me? I'm a good person. Why do they need more info? They already gave me my bad news. Are they looking for more?* The more I thought, the more my answers got distorted. The more the answers twisted up in my head, the more I felt like I was suffocating—like someone had put the covers over my head and I couldn't get enough air in my lungs. My body also had a weird, slight shake, like I had Parkinson's or something. That freaked me out even more. At that point, I knew sleep was just not in the cards, no matter what I took. If you can't shut off your mind, you can't shut down the body.

Finally, the alarm went off. Bob got up, and off we went.

The Big Test

Here's the good news: I had an option of being given something to take the edge off. I thought long and hard about this. The day before, I'd asked the doctor how the procedure worked. I said, "Explain to me the process."

He told me what would happen, step by step. He also was very kind. He must have sensed my incredible fear, because he assured me that he would personally perform my procedure. This was unheard of; he was the head of the oncology department. All this reassured me that I could do the test awake with no drugs. I also thought that if I could deliver a baby with absolutely no drugs (foolish me) and be in labor for twenty-something hours, enduring the most horrific pain imaginable — like being stabbed a million times in a row with no break — I could stand a twenty-minute procedure.

My doctor told me I would get some local anesthesia, so at least I would be somewhat numb.

Prep time. Pretty easy stuff. Pull down your pants. Lie on your belly and have eight people starring at your back end. The procedure began. Bob stood at the front of the table so he could rub my head, but he was also trying to watch what was happening. They first had to numb my ass, and just as I felt the needle go in, I saw Bob turn white as a sheet. They had to be using the longest needle they could find. I wanted to joke "my ass isn't that big," but I had to concentrate on my breathing instead of making wisecracks.

From that point, they need some sort of drill to penetrate the bone and then aspirate the marrow. The doctor tries to prepare me, and I took a long Pilates breath. The pain I felt put childbirth in the easy-as-cake category. After what seems like an awfully long time, the drill stopped. But there was a problem. The head of oncology said, "I didn't get what I need. We need to do it again."

I looked up at my doctor, who was sweating profusely and said, "You're joking."

Another couple of long Pilates breaths. Fortunately, I had learned long ago that we do have some control over pain. The mind is powerful. When I'm in a physically painful situation, I go to another place. I call it my happy place. I also knew I needed to get through that test, and I was going to give it the best breath work I knew. I'd learned a lot of breath patterns in Lamaze, and twenty years later with all my Pilates training, I was going to breathe that pain away. And I did. One small victory!

Good thing: second time was the charm. As the doctor drew out the needle and proclaimed his success, I thought, *All right, I conquered another test!* It was another small victory. I was thrilled — at least for the few hours before we got the results back.

When we reconvened, the doctor, while kind, was also very much to the point. He said, "Mrs. Beck, you have non-Hodgkin B-cell chronic slow-moving marginal-cell lymphoma." Digest that one if you will. What happened to my simple leukemia? *I want that one back,* I thought. *It's much easier to remember.*

I had lots of questions for the doc. What did all that gobbley-goop mean? He stated, "Well, to be honest, I have not seen this in a long time. You have a rare form, and we do not usually see this in a woman your age."

Rare…Don't see…My age. Looks like three strikes and you're out. At that point I had totally checked out. *What's the point of continuing on? Just to hear more disturbing news?*

All right, I give. I had another question. "How often do you see what I have?"

The doctor said, "Well, to be honest, about five cases in fifteen years." Definitely not good. We're in one of the best cancer hospitals in this part of the country.

Next question: "So, what do you advise from this point forward?"

"We need to do a CT scan [oh no, not another scary test], and I would advise chemo."

"Really? What kind?" Like I know the different formulas.

"We would do the CHOP."

I found out later that chemo doesn't get any more potent than that.

Since I didn't know what a CHOP was at that point, I decide to be cautious. "How long do I have before I make this decision?"

"Well, I would go home and enjoy your Easter holiday. Get all your affairs in order, and prepare for the next week."

Basically, he was giving me two to three weeks. I had Bob tape the whole conversation, because I didn't want to miss anything. But he didn't need to. I can still hear it all clearly in my mind.

I thanked the doctor and absorbed what I could. I knew I was in the fight of my life. I was going to have to fight *for* my life. At that time, I had no idea what weapons I possessed.

Intuition
Chapter 3

To Chemo or Not to Chemo

The first person I called when I got back from cancer hospital was Mom. After I first told her my news, we went from practically not talking at all to her phoning me three to four times a day. It didn't matter what city Mom was in, she called.

I gave her the latest news, and she listened. Just listened. She didn't judge; she didn't accuse. I did plenty of that for her. In the back of my sick mind, I was telling myself that I had finally gotten what I deserved. Up to the time of my diagnosis, my wonderful husband and I had been fighting more and more. My mother and Grannie had told me I was a difficult child. I was ornery, angry, and stubborn—all those things I wasn't supposed to be. For the millionth time, I played out the events that led up to our estrangement.

Grannie was eighty-nine when she came to live with me. I begged her to come. She had recently been diagnosed with Parkinson's and was having a lot of balancing issues. She usually spent the winters with me, because I had a beautiful home in Atlanta, and I didn't want her to be alone in New York. When she started losing her mind to Alzheimer's, I convinced her it was time. I also promised her she would never be put in a nursing home.

When Grannie moved in, I added a cantankerous old woman to my brood of three very active adolescent boys—Bob's son and my two. Even though Bob and I were fighting a lot in those days, he agreed to take my granny in. He knew how much I loved her and how much I wanted to give back to her; for all her faults and foibles, she had practically raised me. I did everything I could for her. I bathed her, cooked with her, took her everywhere with me. I got a wheelchair so that I could take her on my power walks. I took her to the stables so she could be there while I taught my lessons and then took her to horse shows—anything to keep her entertained.

In the middle of the night, Grannie would fall out of bed, screaming for someone to come rescue her. I put a baby monitor in her room so that I could hear her if something happened. I moved her to a bedroom near the boys. They would help her unhook her bra, brush her teeth, even put on her clothes at times. We all took part in her care. We gave our hearts to her.

When she was ninety-two, I decided that it was time for her to visit her daughter, my mom. At that point, Grannie had been living with us for three years. Every day she would ask me, "Why doesn't your mom come and visit me?"

I didn't know what to tell her. I just made excuses: "Grannie, it's hard for you to travel, and Mom's schedule is so busy, she can't just drop everything to come visit." That just added to the smoldering anger I had with my mother. There she was again, putting her career ahead of her family.

But I finally decided that I'd had enough. It was time for Grannie to go see her daughter for a couple of weeks. I arranged for a nurse to fly with her and stay with them both for the duration of the visit. What I didn't know was that Grannie had been planning her escape. By this point, Alzheimer's had done its dirty work, so that not only was Grannie losing her memory, she was also being irrational. During her visit, she started telling Mom lies about her money.

Grannie was very attached to her money. You would think she had a multimillion-dollar fortune stashed away. She had saved all her life and was maybe worth 600,000. She had told me long before that she wanted to leave everything to her grandchildren. She felt we were more a part of her life than her only child. I told her that was not a good plan and that it wasn't Mom's fault that she had to work so hard to maintain her lifestyle. I would ask Grannie, "Why should she be punished for this?" But she could never give me a real answer.

One day, something shifted in my grandmother; she became very suspicious of me — another manifestation of her disease. She started thinking I was stealing her money, even though she had put me in charge of all her finances. She had a small Social Security check coming in every month and had some stock that paid her dividends. Most of her estate was in her home, and that was free and clear. That home had so many memories for me and my brothers, and she wanted us to have it because we had spent so much time there. My mom, on the other hand, spent very little time there.

When she first moved in with me, Grannie insisted that I have power of attorney over her estate, instead of her daughter. I said no. I would only do it if Mom were on the document as well, and so she relented. As time went on, Grannie started calling her attorney every other month and changing her will according to her feelings. It was total madness. She had become totally possessed about her money.

When she went to visit my mom, she told such lies that I was literally sick to my stomach. I couldn't believe it — this was the thanks I got after I sacrificed my life for three years, day in and day out, to take care of her? In any case, I was glad to take care of her.

The lies and confusion over where her money went became very convoluted. To make matters worse, Mom's husband, who was cheating on her at the time, got involved as well. I couldn't help but think how awful it was that he was cheating on my mom, trying to decide when to exit her life, and getting all involved in my grandmother's finances. Maybe it was to cover up his own sins. Twenty years prior, he had borrowed twenty thousand dollars from Grannie and never paid her back.

My whole family turned against me except my dad. He believed me. Fortunately, he knew what was going on, based on a visit to our home in Georgia. He had spent only a few nights with me and Grannie, but I guess it was enough to know the truth.

At that point, I decided to retreat. I was devastated that I was being accused of such lies. My belief is, if you have to defend yourself, you're guilty. That's when I stopped talking to my mother and brothers. Dad was the only one I still communicated with. But every day for three years, this ate away at me like a fungus. It was a parasite of anger and sadness, and at least once a day I would think about it, and it would create a deep hurt down to my bones. I felt so heavy every day. Here I had this wonderful life, living in a country-club community, playing tennis, raising my family, but I never quite felt happy.

Grannie moved in with Mom. I felt abandoned and hurt. Six months after she moved in, Mom couldn't take it and put Grannie in a nursing home. It was so ironic: Grannie spent her life resisting the idea of living out her life in a nursing home, and there she was, all alone. The nursing home expenses ate through her estate in about five years. Her favorite saying was, "I'm saving my money for when I get old." While her words held true, I still felt I had failed her and my family. Above all, I had failed myself. It's funny how much you can pack into a couple of thoughts that last only a few seconds.

War and Peace

As I waited for my mom to say something after I told her the news, I thought of the recent past. Did I ever believe in my wildest dreams that my mom would become one with me? I guess in some crazy, unconscious way this was my dream, but it was now my reality. When Mom divorced my dad, I didn't do so well emotionally. The way I saw it, I was shipped off to boarding school so Mom could start her new life. Grannie aside, I had been angry at my mom for more than twenty years, and our relationship was a constant struggle.

When I made that first phone call to Mom, I felt as if the past had been erased, and all that mattered was getting well.

After what seemed like forever, but was probably only a few seconds, she finally said something about my news. She told me she had a plan. She would fly me to Boston on her dime (that in itself was a very big deal), and I would see the top lymphoma doctor at Dana Farber — one of the top cancer centers in the country. Sounded good to me.

But, oh no, this began an all-out war between my husband and my mother. Bob thought the news we got at the Cancer Hospital was good enough. Bob is a hard worker and a provider, and he wants things handled fast. He's a fixer. Fix it fast and efficiently. That's why companies hire him as a consultant to "fix what's wrong." He wanted me to get chemo and be done with it.

My mom started pushing me to go to Boston. She said, "You need a second opinion."

Bob started pulling harder the other way. He said, "Boston is too far away." And he disliked my mother, so why listen to her? Without me knowing it, they were waging their own war of hate mail via the Internet. I'm listening to Dr. Oz, who says get a second opinion. Like anyone who has just been diagnosed with cancer, I was getting a lot of pressure from my family. Fortunately, I didn't know what was going on between my mother and husband. I had my own war to fight at the cellular level. I'm so glad they kept it to themselves. I was thinking I had about six months at that point. I wanted to enjoy my time.

As all the hate mail was flying back and forth, Mom called me every day and said, "I'll pay for the ticket. Please, just come."

Bob figured out his own backup plan. He decided I needed to get a second opinion locally. I got a referral from my first cancer doctor for another cancer specialist close by, only an hour's drive from our house. The two doctors had known each other for years. I also found out his wife passed away from non-Hodgkin's lymphoma. Great endorsement. But I was tired, and I didn't want this to go on and on, so I told Bob I'd go with him. I was a little miffed because I knew my husband. He wanted to stay local so it would be convenient. He also knew I was beyond deathly afraid to fly. He got me on that one.

As we wait for the appointment in Pensacola, I was still not sure what was best. I had been doing my homework and found out what non-Hodgkin's is. It's not a simple cancer; it's not contained to one area of the body. It's called systemic, which means it's everywhere in the body. It's a cancer that affects your lymphatic system, which is basically your cleaning-out system. For example, your tonsils are part of it. Lymph is a fluid that pumps through your body just like your blood. It stops for cleaning at various places along the body in some-thing called lymph nodes, little bean-shaped nodes in places like in your armpits, in your throat, and in your groin that continually flush out toxins — if all is functioning well. If they aren't functioning well, they get clogged. The nodes enlarge and can't do their job — that's why my spleen was so enlarged as well as my stomach — and the body quickly becomes full of toxins.

When the lymph node is clogged — say with cancer — then the lymph can't do its job either, which is to help keep the body at optimum levels of functioning. This type of cancer is practi-cally impossible to treat, because it is systemic. It's not concen-trated in just one area like a breast or a prostate gland. There are also thirty-two known types of this kind of cancer. Worst of all, you can't cut it out. According to Western medicine, you can only try to get rid of some of it with chemo — and that's not really helpful, because this type of lymphoma goes into a dor-mant remission and appears again. Supposedly, it never fully leaves your body.

To make matters worse, I also had leukemia, which is a blood cancer, which again means it's everywhere in the body. Blood is made up of white cells and red cells. Your white cells help to fight off disease, but your red are equally as important. Leukemia affects the production of white cells. They overproduce.

I had blood and lymph cancer, so what should I choose? Convenience, even though the hospital an hour away was supposed to be state of the art? Or an expert in this particular type of lymphoma at the best institution possible—the doctor at Dana Farber, the hospital up in Boston. Bob won that round. We made the trip to the hospital that was close to home.

Opinion 9

Bob and I met with the doctor. After going through all the blood work, he confirmed that chemo was the best option. He also confirmed what I had found in my research: there are no guarantees. Our second opinion told us, "We have not found a cure for this type of cancer—unlike breast cancer, where there is a 98 percent cure rate if caught in time." But the doctor did say, "There is always the exception though." While I'm concentrating on the "exception" part, Bob was happy. He had confirmation by two doctors. He said, "Let's go here. It's only an hour drive from the house. Boston isn't necessary. Your mom is just trying to butt in."

Being an ex-football player and the author of a football book, Bob then basically said I needed to pull on my cleats, strap on my helmet, put in my mouthpiece, and get in the game to win.

It was all looking very bleak, but there was something else. None of this made sense. I was in total denial. I didn't believe that I had what they told me. It just wasn't possible. Looking back, I realize that was why I kept looking for more answers, kept going to the next place. In the midst of all the other chatter in my head, I kept saying, *This isn't true. It's not really true.* It didn't matter that I had blood test after blood test as well as the painful bone marrow tests. I still didn't believe.

It finally came down to me to make a decision. Mom kept telling me to do acupuncture, get massages, and go to Boston. I still didn't get the whole acupuncture thing. But I did know she had lots of connections in the health field and had also written a chapter in a wellness journal book, along with seven other books. Then there's my husband with the chemo and the football helmets. My darling wanted me to do chemo for several reasons. That's all he knew based on what he was hearing from the doctors. To him, chemo was my only option.

I finally made *my* decision. I was going to Boston. What did I have to lose? My diagnosis was getting worse with each doctor I went to. If the third doctor confirmed what the other two had already told me, maybe I would finally believe it.

The War Continues

Wow, did I stir up a bunch of crap. I was going against my husband's wishes. He had been my caretaker, hero, and supporter and had been there emotionally — probably too emotionally. He knew the family history between my mother and me. It was like I was giving him the finger. "Thanks, honey, for all that you've done. I'm outta here."

I tried to explain. "I know you hate my mom. True, I haven't gotten along with her since we've been together, but something is telling me to give her this chance. Trust her, believe that she may have a better solution, respect her knowledge and connections. Give her this one chance to step up to the plate and be a mother for once." I realize now that this was a potential cause for divorce. But I had to go with my gut instinct. I decided the two of them had to put their power guns away and help me do what I was being pulled to do.

While I was making plans to go to Boston, Bob wasn't ready to give up. He was determined that I was going to get chemo and beat this thing; he couldn't hear that the chemo wasn't going to work. He wanted the cancer out of my body. He was losing his mother to cancer; he wasn't ready to let his wife go too. He did everything he could to keep me from going to Boston. He fought. He cajoled. He told me that he didn't trust my mother to follow through, because she was unavailable all those years. Out of respect for him, I decided to try it his way.

Back we go to the hospital that's close to our home. I walked in, and immediately I was uneasy. It didn't feel state of the art. I felt like I was in some facility that was not operating at its highest potential. I was taught that you should always find the best care when it comes to your health. I wasn't feeling it there. Everything appeared outdated.

I also had my guard up. I didn't know exactly how I wanted to be treated, but the people there didn't seem warm and welcoming. When I met with the doctor, there was a disconnect. I felt like he was following a made-for-TV movie script. He wasn't looking at me like I was person. Again, I felt like a number, being identified by my disease. It didn't matter to him that I had a family who loved me, a life full of promise that I wanted to live. Boston was looking better and better.

When we left the meeting, I was whisked over to the part of the hospital where they were supposed to insert a port—the tube that would feed the chemo into my body. Bob knew me well. He didn't want me to have time to think, so he already had the appointment set up. The procedure sounded barbaric: they insert a tube just under your left clavicle. I understand why they do it, but the thought of some device inserted in my body for the duration of the treatment didn't feel right. Strike two. Then, when we went up to the counter to check in, I again felt like a number, not a person. Just like with the doctor, I felt like they were just going through the motions—move 'em in, move 'em out. Strike three, but I wasn't out. Not quite yet.

I asked to see where they did the chemo. Everybody was sitting in a circle in ugly, old recliners. I understood the hospital was trying to provide a homey, comfortable atmosphere, but I recoiled. I don't do ugly; cancer is ugly. I couldn't wrap my mind around the whole idea of it. These people were sitting around like they were at a campfire while they were being infused with poison disguised as medicine. And they all looked like they were dying.

That was the final strike. At that moment I started thinking, *Why would I do this when they're saying it doesn't work for my condition? That's just madness.* Then I had another, familiar, crazy thought, *What if they put me to sleep to put in this crazy port, and I die from just doing that? These people here just do not look competent to handle this.* While all these thoughts were whirling around, something inside just kept saying *no!* I wasn't feeling it. Poor Bob was trying to be patient. I know he thought that this was the right thing to do, but at that point he had his head in the sand. Bob knew what Bob wanted to know. He had no interest in exploring other things.

But I knew that if I stayed there, I would die, and I wasn't ready to do that. I gently, but firmly, told my darling husband that we were going home.

"No we're not," he said in his most authoritative voice. He's a big guy, and he can be pretty authoritative when he wants.

"Yes, we are. I don't like this. I don't like how it feels. I'm going to Boston."

I must have given Bob a look, because he didn't fight. He did say that he wouldn't go with me, because someone needed to stay home with the boys. I think he just didn't want to deal with my mother.

A Most Intriguing Detour

It took everything I had to get on that plane alone, but I did. The plane didn't crash (even though I kept thinking it would), and I got to Boston. Mom and I took a detour before going to the Dana Farber Cancer Institute. It turned out to be a pivotal detour, because it opened up a whole new world to me, one that I never knew existed and one that was to become an integral part of my healing journey.

When I get to Boston, Mom told me that we were first going to visit her Reiki master. "Reeekee what?" I ask. I had vaguely heard of it before and thought it was some kind of massage. I have mixed feelings about massage. Some of the research suggested that it could help spread the lymphoma. She looked like she was about to lecture me but then changed her mind.

"It's all about healing energy," she said. "You don't have to say a word, and the Reiki master won't even touch you." I didn't know what to say, so I said nothing.

We were greeted at the door by the sweetest woman. That instantly made me feel good, especially with the Pensacola hospital still fresh in my mind. We talked briefly. I filled out my paperwork and thought, *Here I go.*

The woman told me not to take off my clothes. I thought this was odd, but didn't say anything. She said to lie on the table face up. I closed my eyes, just trying to relax my mind. It was the first time I'd even thought about relaxing. It was *almost* fun. Just two weeks before, I had discovered I had an incurable disease. I wasn't even sure how bad the cancer was; my diagnosis kept changing. It seems like ages since I'd first found out.

The Reiki master stood over my head for quite a while. I wanted to open my eyes, but I didn't want to disturb whatever she was doing. After about ten minutes, she traveled to my neck area, with her hands floating over my body. She shifted to my stomach area and stopped. She spent the rest of the time focusing on that area of my body. She particularly stayed on the left side of my body. I kept thinking, *Boy, this is weird. What is she doing?* She was just moving her hands above my body. I was starting to wonder why I listened to my mom. As she finishes, she said, "I'm now going to burn some sage." At that point, I thought, *Whatever you think. Maybe we can burn it out of my body with herbs.* Then I thought, *It can't get much weirder than this. I'll just go with the flow.*

When she was done doing whatever it was she did with the sage, she proceeded to let me know some concerns and what she'd felt. This was funny to me. How in God's name could she have concerns because she felt certain things going on in my body? She never touched me! Boy, was I feeling foolish. I started berating myself that I'd allowed the treatment to even go to completion. I said, "Okay, tell me what you felt and didn't feel."

She said, "I feel a lot of heat around the left side of your belly. It's so strong, I couldn't move my hands away." Now she had my attention, so I listened carefully. I still fought the urge to run. She also said that she felt heat in my groin area and in my lungs. Here's the crazy thing: at the time my spleen was extremely enlarged, and I had tumors in my lung region. My lymph nodes were also swollen in my groin. This woman had no idea of any of that. I'm sure Mumsie mentioned I was diagnosed with cancer, but I know that she didn't give details, because we were so uncertain ourselves. I looked at the Reiki master hard and then thanked her. As I was leaving, I felt a sense of peace I hadn't felt since I started noticing the rashes on my body.

Watchful Waiting

Our next stop was the Dana Farber Cancer Institute. I expected the same horrible experience that I'd had at Pensacola hospital close to our home. Bob's words floated through my mind: "You know Boston is old, the weather is nasty, and the people are arrogant." He had been using every trick he knew to keep me home.

When I walked through the automatic doors of Dana Farber, I felt a sense of relief, almost like I was home. It was welcoming. People smiled and called me by name. I felt like I was at a "cancer spa" to get help and healthy. When it was time to draw my blood, the nurse put a pillow under my arm, asked me how I was doing, and smiled reassuringly. She noticed my veins were tiny and found a smaller needle. My mind said, *I am safe here. I am safe.* I took a deep breath and was hopeful.

It was time to meet The Doctor. After my vitals were taken, Mom and I were sent to a small waiting room. We waited. And waited. I started to feel panicky. Finally, Dr. Fisher entered the room, but not alone. *Why is there another doctor with him?* My mind started racing with all sorts of doomsday ideas. I stopped, and when I took a good look at Dr. Fisher, he looked like a big Teddy bear who had come for a visit. He had a beard, a pleasant manner, and a peaceful presence. He shook my hand and then sat in his chair. He leaned back slightly, very casually, and asked, "So, how do you feel?"

I swallowed hard. "I am hearing *that* question a lot." We both chuckled, which made me feel a little overly sarcastic. "Well, I used to feel good, until I was told I had some rare, chronic, no-cure disease that seems to be getting worse each time I go to a different doctor."

He smiled. "Well, the tests do confirm that you have non-Hodgkin's."

I guess I needed to believe it, since now *three* doctors had confirmed it. "So, what are my options?" I didn't know if I was ready to hear the answer. *It can't be good.*

A bit more somberly, Dr. Fisher said, "Not too many."

Mom and I looked at each other. My whole world went silent.

"Okay, let me ask you this," I said. "If you were in my shoes, what would you do?"

"Well," he said, "we need to save your magic bullets."

I didn't ask what those magic bullets were. All I said was, "Awesome! Somebody is going to give me magic bullets! And I will be back to normal again?"

"Not quite. The magic bullet is chemo, and it's anything but magic. Stopgap is more like it. This disease is considered chronic. Chemo might get rid of it for a while, but there's a good chance it will return."

In some strange, desperate way, this was good news. It gave me time to explore and learn what affect chemo has on the body, especially a forty-two-year-old body. Chemo basically destroys all the good cells in the body while trying to terminate the bad cells. It weakens your immune system, leaving you extremely vulnerable. This wasn't good, since my immune system was already weak at the time. The chemo cocktail protocol was considered the strongest and most potent available. I also learned that the concoctions couldn't be administered repeatedly. *Ah, no wonder Dr. Fisher calls them the magic bullets. You load the gun, take a shot, and it's hit or miss.*

I asked, "How many cases are you seeing a year like mine?"

"We treat between two hundred and three hundred cases a year."

I thought, *That's much better odds than five cases in fifteen years. He must know what he's doing.* I'd finally found someone I could trust. I was beginning to feel better.

"So, Doc," I asked, "what do we do?"

He asks me again, "How do you feel?"

I cocked my head. *Is this a trick question?* He smiled and clarified his question. "Do you have night sweats? Have you lost a lot of weight lately, and do you feel extremely tired?"

I paused in thought. "Not really." I felt tired, but not extremely. I didn't have night sweats, and I'd lost weight because I couldn't eat due to nerves. I guess I gave the right answer, because he told me I could go home.

"We're sending you home to do what's called 'watchful waiting.' In other words, we aren't going to do anything for the moment; we're all going to just wait to see what happens."

Okay, we wait. I was worried, but agreed chemo was a last resort.

Dr. Fisher said, "Come back in three months. We'll do your blood work again and a CT scan." I promised to return in three months, and we left the room.

I wasn't thrilled about the CT scan, but at least I didn't have to do chemo. I called Bob with the news, and I wasn't sure if he was happy or disappointed. He was losing his mother, and he had decided that chemo was the way to go. His only negative comment was, "Are they waiting for you to get really sick?"

Saying Good-bye

Bob's mom died two weeks after I returned from Boston. It was devastating, even though we knew she was dying. I had a rocky relationship with Bob's mom, whom we called Momma Dee. She was his biggest cheerleader and fan. She adored everything about Bob to a fault. I know she resented me when I came into the picture. She tried so hard to dislike me.

At first, she made lots of waves; she made it very clear that she was number one in Bob's world. Being a good wife to my new husband, I tried so hard to treat her well. Wanting to please Bob and Momma Dee, I gave it my all and stuffed my feelings. The harder I tried, the madder I made her. Her intense dislike for me lasted almost ten years. She was determined to make sure I didn't forget it.

Then one day we had a come-to-Jesus, knock-down, verbal fight. I felt terrible, since I was the only one who spoke. And I shared my feelings, which was hard for me. I let her know that she never made me feel special. I told her I knew she resented me, and I asked her why she felt so angry. I told her, "I want you to know I encourage Bob to be a good son and do everything we can to help you. I just want a chance to be a good daughter to you too." This began our healing journey, opening dialogue and our hearts. Dee and I became close. Thank God that happened before she got sick. I laugh at the irony that I started to hang out with Momma Dee more than with Bob. We chatted for hours and drank wine. I grew to love Momma-Dee and took care of her like Grannie.

When I opened my Pilates studio at the beach, Dee helped me run it. I was always trying to get her out and about. I felt it was important that she was around people. When Dee was diagnosed with lung cancer, no one was surprised, because of her long-time smoking habit. It made me sad, because we had become so close. I looked forward to our weekly talks, our lunches, our toenail polishing. Bob was always the subject of our conversation. Whatever Bob-bashing we did, it was in a loving way. We both loved him dearly. It was our common bond.

When she began her treatments, Bob was her primary caregiver. He was starting his own consulting business after years in the corporate world. His timing was perfect for taking care of Momma Dee. Bob was amazing—he took her grocery shopping, something he had *never* attempted. Meeting Dee's needs took most of Bob's time and energy, but I was perfectly fine with that. After all, she had cancer.

When I was first diagnosed, Bob and I had Sunday brunch with Momma Dee. It was horrible, especially for Bob. Dee was terminal, and I was "maybe" "wait and see" terminal. It felt more like a funeral than a meal with Bob's two best girls.

Dee looked right at me and said, "This is not right, but I'm going to make it right. God is not going to take both of us away from him. He needs you to take care of him. He is not meant to be without a woman." Even though Dee and I had become closer, her first concern was always Bob. Maybe Dee thought heaven wasn't big enough for both of us.

Shortly after I returned from Boston, Momma Dee needed to go into hospice. Just before she died, she mustered enough strength to raise her voice. She was on morphine and could barely move. She whispered, "Come here."

She looks at me, her eyes focused and crystal clear, and said, "I will make it right with God. I will make sure you get better. Bob needs you. He loves you more than life. I have had my time on earth, and I'm ready to go. Don't worry, I've got it handled." I squeezed her hand. Thank you, Momma Dee. I don't know how much of my life I owe to you, but I sure feel better knowing I had someone close to God acting on my behalf.

What Do I Have to Lose?

As Momma Dee was preparing for her own journey to heaven, my thoughts and feelings were chaotic. *Am I living, dying, getting worse, or getting better? Am I here for a short time? If so, I'd better enjoy every day like it's my last.* If I were to follow my beloved mother-in-law shortly, I wanted to see as many sunsets as possible. I wanted to see my children every day. I wanted to love my husband as much as possible. I wanted to smell the saltwater. I wanted to see the sun come up in the morning, every morning. I wanted to feel the hope each new day brings. I decided to eat the best meals I could and to walk as often as I could in the fresh air.

I did learn what it means to live in the moment. I made a conscious effort to laugh, sing, and play music. I took time to hang with my girlfriends, drink wine, and share stories. I continued to work with my clients, to love on my dogs, and to experience every second of every minute. I relished all things, because I didn't know how many days I had left. Like most people pondering a death sentence, I decided I would do everything on my bucket list. But first I needed a list. For starters, I wanted to read novels and travel. I realized I had put so many things on hold while raising my children.

I also had an overwhelming desire to become a grandmother — maybe have a girl grandbaby that I would spoil rotten. I'd buy her a pony and teach her to ride. I knew that being a Mimi to a grandbaby was a long shot. Sadness at the idea of never knowing my grandchild was suffocating. I pushed these thoughts away-for now.

And I thought about how I could have lived a better life, been a better human being. I know this all sounds crazy, but it's true. I knew I couldn't go back, and that was okay, but I wanted to find some way to do it over again, to relive the positive, to change any negative impact I had on God's creation. At that moment, my decision is firm. I would do the protocol at Dana Farber Cancer Institute. My journey for survival was in full throttle, and the ride would be a wild one.

Tenacity

CHAPTER 4

Time to Heal

When I made the decision to go to Dana Farber, I knew I faced the challenge of negotiating a deal with Bob. He is a very persuasive, persistent businessman who negotiates for a living and plays to win. That's hardwired in him and one of the things I love about him—most of the time. When I knew I had to negotiate with him, I knew it wasn't going to be easy. But I didn't want to negotiate my decision. So I presented him with an argument that he couldn't debate. If he did, he would be a total jerk—and that's just not his style.

When I got home from Boston, we sat down and had a long talk. We talked about trust, about our fears, and about the uncertainty of the future. I said to my darling hubby, "I don't know what's going to happen in my life. But because this is my life, it's my choice. I need to go with my gut, and you need to honor my decision. It could turn out badly. If it does, at least we both know I made the decision. If you make the decision and it turns out badly, could you live with that?"

What could he say? Typically, Bob isn't ready to respond to my argument. He likes to think through the various scenarios. At 4:30 a.m. the next morning, he sent me an e-mail:

Subject: Good Day Mate

Hey You,

Damn, I have been up since 4:00 am with no reason why. You know what I said tonight was my honest belief about you. I am not even a little surprised that the entire community is calling, e-mailing, offering to do whatever, showing sincere care and love for you. You are a people magnet and they love you. You are so sincere with the most loving heart of anyone I have known or ever will know. I don't think you have always been that way, but over the last few years you have really drawn tons of people to you. Maybe you always have had the gift but because you have been exposed to more people is why so many people are rallying around you.

When you come out on the other end of this journey we are about to embark on, I believe you will be an even better person than you already are! I think it would be impossible to draw more people to you. But I think you won't be as anxious, need the control you want, and loosen up with me a bit. I am excited about that! Maybe when we are empty nesters in a year we can really recapture our twenties since we were parents and had tons of responsibilities then.

Because of what you dealt with growing up, I would think it would be hard to trust any positive feelings you might have gotten from any of your family. So I can understand that it might be hard to trust my sincere love for you too. When we fight like any two people living together for as long as we have, I am sure that just plays into that whole issue. Like I have told you, I HATE that you have to go through this period of sickness but you have been so loving, caring, affectionate, calm it is unbelievable. When you come through the other side, I know you will be all that and more! Hell, you combine that with letting go of some of your fears, control and trust issues, and damn, baby—will you marry me!

Whatever silly questions about my heart or sincere commitment to you will soon be unquestionable (they shouldn't be now but...).

I am looking forward to the next forty years of chasing you around the house and having my way with you! I love you more than life!

Your Husband

My Support System

My husband is in so many ways my rock. I call him my knight in shining armor. I know that I'm the luckiest girl in the world. I never knew that it would take my being so sick to feel so loved. My husband, my mother, my father, my sons—everyone with whom I am close—shower me with such an outpouring of love it overwhelms me to think about it.

I sent Bob the following message:

Subject: RE: Good Day Mate

To my Knight in Shining Armor

I do believe certain things happen for a reason. Whether it turns out good or bad, I will try to find the silver lining in all this. I do feel I have changed instantly; if I could go back in time I will never be the same again. Even though I am scared, I feel stronger. Each day is an emotional challenge, but I have already truly learned how powerful the mind is. It can pick you up or knock you down hard. (Boy, did I learn that was — and is — an understatement. I will do my best to keep my sanity through this emotional rollercoaster! If I do falter a bit, know that I am doing my best, and I may not be myself at times. Nothing you haven't experienced before.

You are the greatest man I will ever know, and I believe we were put here only to complement each other and give back to the universe. I love you more than ever and want to love you for the rest of my life.

Laurie

On this life journey, I've found out how *truly* powerful a kind, caring, support system is. I've also found out that facing death helps people figure out how much love they have in their life and makes them want to love more. That's a cliché perhaps, but it's an absolute truth. I know we would all be better off if we loved each other as if it were our last day on earth.

It did take my husband a little bit more convincing. He insisted that Dr. Fisher send over a full report. Bob tried to talk me into getting a *fourth* opinion at someplace like Mayo or MD Anderson Cancer Center in Houston. He wanted to be 100 percent that we chose the right course of action. He was protecting us. He said, "I don't want you to get too high and excited just to crash if something from today is not quite right." But in the end, he stepped aside and supported my decision. He faltered along the way; we all do. He had to put up with some pretty horrendous and smelly things, but I know he's glad he did. Life isn't always easy, but dying is a lot harder.

Setting Priorities

When I returned home from the hospital in Boston, I was relieved. I had the gift of time. I promised myself and my family that I was going to do my very best to put the cancer into remission. It could remain dormant for a hundred years; it didn't matter. I told Bob,

"I truly believe that God is telling me something, and I will do my best to listen and to try to change so that I can heal."

Being brave and having a positive attitude doesn't mean I didn't slide into a pity party from time to time. My boys and Bob were outside on the deck, laughing and having fun. I was upstairs in my room, crying. While I had a lot of resolve to fight the cancer, I had one-woman pity parties. I was scared of losing everything I loved, and all that I loved was engaged in life on the deck below me. Then I looked at them and had a major aha moment. I realized that they weren't going to stop living because I had cancer. Who wants to mope around all the time? Life should be filled with laughter and joy. But I also decided something. I resented that I put their needs and wants ahead of my needs. No more. I marched out onto the deck, asked them to sit down, and told them, "I have given all of myself to you, but now I need to make it about me. My priority is to get healthy. The boys are going to have to become self-sufficient. It's a big change for all of us." They knew better than to respond when Mom had "the look," and from that moment on, I have a different job to do. I wasn't going to let fear, opinion, or anything negative get in the way of doing the best things to defeat the enemy, cancer.

Step One: Reiki

When Mom told me to get acupuncture, I thought she was crazy. How could that possibly heal me? She explained very quickly, "Acupuncture can alleviate stress in the body." She should know. Mom, a.k.a. Loretta LaRoche, speaks all over the world. Loretta is one of the top motivational speaker-humorists on the subject of stress. No matter what happened in our past, I decided to let go and look at the data. This is my new beginning.

There are many things that cause disease in the body. Cumulative studies are starting to show that stress can cause 70 percent of today's diseases. Stress comes from all areas of life. Seen or unseen, it can be from a tough boss or nasty coworkers, or from having environmental toxins zap your body of its strength. Stress is a fierce foe, but it's manageable. I learned each day a new life lesson. Hate less, love more, and let go.

I had a definitive plan in mind for my treatment. I wasn't going to sit around and wait. I had three months before I would return to the cancer clinic. I decided it was time for me to become active in my recovery. I decided to trust my gut and listen to Mom. They both seemed to be leading me in the right direction. The stress needed to be eradicated from my lifestyle, so the first step was to find a Reiki master. I had felt so calm after the one visit to my mom's practitioner. Since she didn't even touch me, it certainly couldn't do any harm. Five miles from my home, I discover an amazing woman, Janet. She turned out to be the first gem I added to my healing collection.

I call her on the phone and ask a myriad of questions. I told her my diagnosis. She was neither hesitant nor afraid. We talked about Reiki and its benefits. I made my first of many appointments. Each one was the same. After every session, I felt calm. During the first month of watchful waiting, when I was calm, I definitely noticed it. It wasn't easy to be calm.

After she completed each session, we discussed what sensations she experienced, and she sometimes asked if they were the same for me. As I started to feel more comfortable with Janet and her expertise, I became open to suggestions. She was in the learning stages of myofascial release therapy. The fascia is a seamless web of connective tissue that covers and connects the muscles, organs, and skeletal structures. It is between the skin and the underlying structure of muscle and bone. The goal of myofascial release is to loosen fascia restriction and restore tissue health. When there are no restrictions, the body feels in harmony and creates balance. I definitely knew I needed more balance in my life; it seemed like a good a place to start.

As we continued our sessions, I learned what Reiki is all about. It's about self-healing, and it assists on your voyage of inward discovery. I needed all the help I could get to make my journey inward. While I knew a good massage when I got one, Reiki was all very new to me; the treatments and even the very language was foreign. I learned to be quiet and listen. I wasn't about to open my mouth and ruin anything. All I knew was that Reiki helped calm me, and that's all I needed to know at that point. I was on a learning curve.

Step Two: Acupuncture

I didn't realize my healing plan was actually a practice of integrative medicine — integrating Western medicine with alternative therapies. Mom kept pushing acupuncture, and since she was so right about the Reiki thing, I decided to give it a try. At that point, I wasn't looking at those treatments as a way to cure me. I just knew that I felt safe and trusted the people who were caring for me. I continued on my path of letting go.

I was scared to death to have needles, lots of them, inserted all over my body. *Why*, I thought, *would any fool want needles placed from the crown of her head down through to her toes?* The key word here is *fool. I think the cancer must be in my brain.* (Gallows humor.) After all, voodoo doctors stick needles in dolls when you want to create pain in an enemy, right? I was truly ignorant about acupuncture, but I knew I had been ignorant about a lot of other things up to that point. I felt that I had some divine intervention when I got my three months of watchful waiting. I wasn't going to let my fear and ignorance stand in the way of my life. I scheduled my first acupuncture treatment for May 18, 2006.

I walked into the acupuncture clinic, and it was very calm and peaceful in that Zen, feng shui sort of way. I was greeted by calm, serene people. Part of my decision to go with the doctors at Dana Farber was because I knew I wanted to be treated in a certain manner. I didn't know what it was supposed to be, but I knew it had to feel right. It's what kept me looking after I got the second opinion. I always make decisions by how something feels to me. It drives my husband crazy, but my gut or intuition is rarely wrong. It's what made me comfortable with Reiki, so I decided that was a very good sign.

I was taken back to a modest office and introduced to Frank. He was very knowledgeable about Chinese medicine, and he spent time explaining how it all works. It's based on putting the body back into balance or harmony with itself. As he filled out my intake form, he asked me a lot of questions based on the information I had given him on the forms. I handed him my blood work and told him I was diagnosed with non-Hodgkin's lymphoma and leukemia.

He said without emotion, "You have lymphoma?"

"Yep, lucky me." I wasn't sure that I liked his tone. But at least it wasn't condescending — just forthright.

"So, you're not doing chemo at this time."

"No." I shook my head to emphasize the *no*. "My doctor in Boston told me I had three months of what he calls 'watchful waiting.'"

"Why are you here?"

"My mom believes acupuncture will calm my body."

"Aren't you going to do treatment?" I was starting to get a little insulted. I thought I was coming in for acupuncture, not a grilling. I responded, "My doctor doesn't feel that's necessary right now. But I'm here for acupuncture, so let's get going."

He ignored my demand and kept asking questions. He told me more about Chinese medicine and the importance of herbs. After talking with me for about an hour, he looked directly at me and said, "I have worked with this before. I believe that if you drink the formula I will give you when you leave, you can eliminate it from your body."

"That's nice. Don't tell me something you think I want to hear."

"That's not who I am."

I believed him.

After all the dialogue, I was led into a little room with a massage bed. It was very peaceful, with a waterfall in the corner. He had five of six other treatment rooms, and all the doors were closed. I assumed they were full.

The official acupuncturist entered the room. Frank told him where to put the needles, and I listened with all my might. I didn't know anything about acupuncture or the meridian (the channels through which energy flows through the body), so it was all fascinating. I wanted to know what they were going to do to me. I lay on the bed, fully hesitant. Right before they put the needles in, I asked, "What's this going to feel like?" I was so anxious I was trembling.

The acupuncturist said, "It might feel like a bee sting."

I can handle a bee sting, I thought. The guy started inserting needles in my feet and worked his way up my leg. I found out later he was hitting the various meridians for my liver, spleen, lungs—all the organs that were affected by the cancer. Some of the needles felt like a slight bee sting as they entered. Some felt like fire; a couple of pricks almost had me jumping off the table. But I stayed put. My mother had been firm—I needed acupuncture to help me handle the stress, so I was going to do it.

It took the practitioner about fifteen minutes to place the needles. I felt like a pin cushion and could have sworn there were at least fifty needles. I was ready for the needles to be removed immediately. That's when Frank said, "Don't move."

"Why not?" I demanded.

"Don't move your hands or lift your legs. If you do, you'll get a really good sting."

Good information. The mere thought of being stung a million times kept me still. I wouldn't move. But this wasn't easy, because I'm claustrophobic. So I asked Frank, "Can you keep someone close by just in case I freak out?" They were very nice about it and told me they would check on me in ten minutes. I told myself, "Girl, you did the bone marrow biopsy. This is a piece of cake!"

Then they dimmed the lights and left.

Oh crap. I started to panic. There I was, basically pinned to the table like a dead butterfly. I couldn't move my hands or legs. Total darkness. I shivered. *This is what it must feel like to be dead.* I felt like a mummy. I didn't want to yell or disturb the other people in treatment. When they left the room, they'd suggested that I relax. *Are you joking? Relax?* How could I relax under those circumstances?

In a few minutes, my nose started to itch. *What do I do?* I decide to scratch it. I moved my hand and quickly received a sharp, shooting pain down my arm. I wondered if this was Mom's pay-back for all the shenanigans I pulled as a teenager.

But my nose still itched. What was I supposed to do? "Okay, mind," I said, "tell my nose to stop itching." It actually worked! Mind control, the lessons were coming in spurts.

My next thought was, "How can I get through twenty min-utes without losing it?"

I began by breathing deep, focused Pilates breaths. I repeated positive affirmations. If I felt a needle, I said, "This is helping my spleen," or liver or lungs or whatever it was that popped into my mind. Later, the more I learned about energy work, the more I asked a lot of questions as they put the needles in so that I could help them out—help them direct the energy even more.

On this first day, as I lay on the table, I was amazed at the sensations moving through my body. I felt an energy current flowing to certain parts of my body that were sick. Somehow I knew my extremely large spleen was having messages sent to it. I could feel where certain areas were blocked, because it was like electricity was being sent to it. I know I sound crazy. And, personally, I thought they were all a little weird at the clinic. But what did I have to lose? That thought kept me plodding on. The powers that be kept telling me there was no cure, so what were a few needles at that point? After fifteen minutes, Frank came to check on me, and I was very grateful. I was even more grateful when the needles were removed.

When I was finished, I honestly can't say how I felt. I've heard others say they felt amazingly more calm, more centered, more alert, even more alive after their acupuncture. In later treatments, I experienced those sensations, but after the first treatment, I wasn't relaxed—not one bit. I was scared, even more tense, and was actually pumped full of adrenaline. Since that's not what I expected, I decided to do what I always did—take it home and allow it to simmer for a while.

Before I left, the people at the counter handed me a bag of herbs. "What are these?" I asked. I can't imagine the tone I used. I was pretty freaked, ready to run out the door.

The assistant simply smiles and said, "Those are your herbs."

"I came for acupuncture, not herbs," I snapped back. I was freaked out. This Frank guy wanted me to drink a bag of smelly herbs. I couldn't even pronounce what they were; all of the writing was in Chinese—literally!

These wonderfully kind people kept smiling at me and nodding. "We know, but you need to drink thirty ounces of tea a day. Directions are inside the bag."

I smiled back and said to myself, "Yeah, right. I will go along and take the herbs this time." I was so cynical. I figured this was just another way for them to make more money off the desperation of a dying cancer patient. My pity-me meter was at an all-time high.

I went home, very curious about what was in the bag, but not sure what to do. Frank's words haunted me: "If you follow my program, you can eliminate it from your body." There was something very powerful about Frank's demeanor. He was very calm and confident. I decided to hear my inner voice inside me. I brewed the herbs.

Paybacks

Herbalicious the herbs were not. They were disgusting and smelly. I never knew something that was so good for you could taste so horrible. I knew nothing about herbs or Chinese medicine. So I asked the same old question, *What do I have to lose?* I certainly didn't want to go back to Boston in three months and undergo the poisonous chemotherapy.

I wasn't sure this was the right course of action. Was Frank a kook or charlatan with his magic potions? I did some research. I found other people who have been to the clinic. I asked a lot of questions about Frank and the clinic. When I mentioned his name, the person listening only had amazing things to say. I talked to one guy who had lymphoma as well, though a different type. We talk for two hours. He said that he tried the herbs for a short time and quit. He simply couldn't swallow them. The good news was it didn't kill him.

I even discovered that Momma Dee had gone to a Chinese doctor. He gave her herbs to help her stop smoking. The boiled herbs tasted so bad, she decided that she would rather smoke than drink the stuff. Well, smoking did kill her. What I didn't understand — and still don't — was how we had never heard about Frank if so many people knew him and were treated by him? I guess the teacher appears when the student is willing. Another lesson clicked into my subconscious.

After two days of hemming and hawing, I thought, *Let's get this party started. I'm in stage-three lymphoma. It could easily slide into stage four.* That old feeling of "what do I have to lose?" came over me once again. I started laughing when I open the bag. They'd also sent me home with a special blue pot too, so it looked like I should be camping and be singing campfire songs while brewing the magic tea. I didn't understand that it was medicine. I quelled the urge to start singing and began brewing my special concoction.

The directions were simple enough: sixty-four ounces of water. Soak the bag of herbs for two hours, simmer at a very low heat for forty-five minutes. Let sit for another two hours or so. Drink warm. Easy, easy. So far so good.

The smell alone was enough to make my dogs leave the room. My youngest son, Nick, walked through the door and asked who died. It did smell, but I didn't need all the undesirable comments. I was thinking, *Thanks for the support, troops! I have to drink this stuff!*

I got my cup ready for action. I took one sip and literally spit it out. I had been warned, but nothing could have prepared me for that taste. It was horrific.

Drinking the tea was not going to be easy, but something told me to persist. I tried everything — holding my nose, taking big sips, taking small sips. I called the clinic and told them my dilemma. They said to try using a straw and to eat three raisins when I was finished. That didn't help either.

Do they really think I'm going to drink thirty ounces of this poison a day? I don't think so. But I kept at it. I decided to drink it in stages. The fact that I decide to persist is shocking to me.

Typically, if I don't know what's in something or have never experienced it, I'm hesitant. As I started taking my tea in small sips, in stages, I wondered if it would alter my thinking, create hallucinations, or just plain kill me. *Hey, maybe that's the joke. It's just speeding up the process so I won't have to experience the last stages of the cancer.*

The first week, I choked down one bag. Phew, only two to go. I decided to get creative. I added a little pomegranate juice to jazz it up. When I shared with Frank's assistant how proud I was that I'd gotten the tea down by spicing it up a little, he let me know I couldn't do that. "You have to drink it in its pure state," he stated, "or else it will change the formula."

I entreated, "I don't care. It tastes better that way." He gave me a look and sent out the big man. Frank entered the room.

I smile sweetly and said, "Frank, I can deal with the acupuncture, but I just can't do the tea."

He looked at me and said, "Do you want to get well?"

I thought, *What a pompous ass.* I almost screamed, "No, I want to get worse. I'm enjoying all my sympathy phone calls — every day with the same questions." I knew it was out of love and concern that everyone was calling me, but what does one say to someone who has an incurable disease? I hated being put in that situation. Whenever someone called, I kept the conversations short and sweet, but it was getting tougher all the time.

At that moment, I wasn't sure whether to like Frank or hate him. Something about him said to drink the tea. I hated the tea but decided to trust Frank. What did I have to lose at that point? So I drank the tea.

My tea became my mission. Suddenly, drinking my tea was a part of me. I can't explain why. It wasn't an easy regime, believe me — brewing, soaking, straining, carrying this stuff wherever I went. It smelled terrible and tasted equally as bad. The worst part — sort of — was that by three in the afternoon, every afternoon, I had the worst gas imaginable. I chose to stay home from three onward so as not to offend anybody. I admit, it's fun getting back at teenage boys and my husband for all the years of "lethal" gas that they exposed me too. *Ha! One silver lining.* I would take as many as I could get. I reminded myself I was living in the moment, finding joy even in a daily gas explosion.

The Whole-Body Concept

At times I felt the only person who fully supported me during the first three months was my mother. She understood the power of the alternative therapies I chose to use. We talked three or four times a day. The nonbelievers were most likely buzzing around behind my back. They smiled at me when I told them what I was doing, but I'm sure they believed I was grasping at whatever I could.

I ask Frank about the herbs when I went in for my weekly acupuncture appointment. He told me the formula I was drinking was for my liver. "There's an imbalance going on there," he said, "and we need to support your liver to make it stronger, because in Chinese medicine, your liver and your spleen are yin and yang. In other words, they are intimately connected." Since my spleen was bulging out of my stomach at that point, my feelings told me this made sense. I had never looked at my body that way. Up to that point, I didn't know what each organ did and which supported what. In Chinese medicine, the body is considered a whole, not just parts, and the key is to look at the root causes of things, not just the symptoms.

The more I learned, the more I was determined to drink my tea—thirty ounces every day. Before long, crazy things started happening to my body. I had continual sores on my body and big canker sores in my mouth and on my tongue. I had herpes on my lips, rashes on my elbows, and a distended belly that made me look three months pregnant. While Bob worked very hard to be supportive, especially with all the side effects going on, every once in a while he would just stare at me and ask, "Are you sure about this?"

"No, honey, I'm not sure about anything anymore, but something is telling me to drink this stuff."

Sometimes he got frustrated. He'd say things like, "Why can't you just do chemo and be done with it?" He still didn't get it. I explained to him again that chemo held no guarantees. I reminded him that there was no cure for this type of cancer. The best I could do was push it back into a latent state. That was the only goal I was focusing on at that point.

I sometimes remembered what Momma Dee had to endure. I woke up in the middle of the night, my mind racing, asking questions. *Am I getting better? Am I getting worse? How long do I have? Why is my spleen still swollen? Are other organs swelling in my body? How can I leave my children behind? They have already had so much heartache.* I woke Bob up, and he listened. We talked. We decided that, if it was my time to go, my boys would be in good hands. I knew Bob would always be there for them, and my mom and dad would help guide them through their adult years. But then I cried, because I thought again of all that I had to lose. Through all of that, something in me kept screaming, "Drink the tea! Drink the tea!" So I drank tea like crazy.

I became fanatical about what I eat. Everything organic. I researched to find the best foods for me. It took me at least three hours to shop. I'd tell Bob, "Honey, I'm going to the store."

He'd shout back, "I'll see you tomorrow." He was never sure what he was going to eat for dinner, but being the trooper he was, he ate his daily rations like a conscripted soldier.

Who was strapping on the helmet at that point, I'm not sure. I do know that my healing journey became a team effort. A wise man once said that a group becomes a team when they face adversity. We were all up against it, and I was calling the shots. What I didn't know was that the hardest and yet the most fulfilling part of my journey was still to come.

Find Serenity

CHAPTER 5

Energy Healing

Cancer is a curious disease. Most disease is caused by cells degenerating or something like bacteria that gets into the cells and kills them. Cancer is different in that it is cells gone renegade. They overproduce; the body's immune response doesn't recognize that there is a problem, so it doesn't work to kill off the excess. I read some very interesting research that suggested the root cause of most cancer, especially the kind that creates tumors, is a wound or a virus or some sort of parasitic or yeast infection, or even a chemical toxicity. The protein markers—the ones they look for in the cancer tests—start surrounding the affected area to kill the infection. The infection persists, and so cells start proliferating rapidly around the infection to contain it. Something snaps, and the cells go crazy. Perhaps it's too simplistic, but it seems like a possible physiological explanation of cancer.

I believe cancer is as much a spiritual malaise as it is a physical disease. Some have even suggested that cancer is a manifestation of problems in the family dynamic. I agree, given what I've been through to get well.

Enter Alice

When the word got out that I had cancer, my mailbox was flooded with cards, letters, postcards. The outpouring of love and concern was overwhelming, but I'm a pessimist. Everyone offered to help, but all I thought was, "What is it you want from me?" Dark thoughts, for sure.

Not long after I had my first acupuncture appointment, I got a card from my neighbor, Alice, who was a longtime client. I didn't know her well, but I always thought she was very nice. The note said, "I think I can help."

Cynical me thought, *Sure you do, and so does everyone else.*

I remembered that Alice did some sort of mind-body-spirit work, so I decided to call her. I'd spent twenty years reading self-help books about mind-body-spirit. And Mom sent me all the latest when she found out I had cancer. While "what do I have to lose" was becoming old hat, it was the very thing that kept me going. I made an appointment to see Alice.

Before I went to my first session, I told Bob. I'm sure he thought, *Poor thing, she's just grasping at anything out there. Let her do her thing for three months, and then the doctors will set her straight.* He never voiced these thoughts, so that might have been my own neurosis about the whole deal, but I could tell he was very impatient. He was in fact scared beyond scared. He still believed the doctors were the only solution.

I started my first session with Alice. We did the usual intake stuff. Then she asked me to lie down on her massage table. And then she started making weird toning noises. I thought, *How am I going to stop myself from laughing? How in God's green earth is this going to help me?*

The answers come slowly. In the end, Alice helped me in many ways. She taught me how to turn darkness into light, change fear into love. She slowly showed me how to visualize health and send love throughout my body. She helped me clean out the negative, unhealthy issues that I held onto as a child.

As I began this journey, I would have never guessed that I would go so deep into myself. The most important gift Alice gave me was allowing me to see that, in order to be well, I needed to learn how to take real responsibility for all the horrible things that happened to me. To heal, I had to learn to let go of the anger I felt toward my ex-husband. I had to learn to forgive my mother, Grannie—anyone whom I thought wronged me. In other words, I had to heal my spirit before I could heal my body.

The "Perfect" Life

I have always been fortunate to live in comfortable circumstances. Before my mom and dad divorced in the early 1970s, I had what outsiders would call a "perfect" life. We had the nice home in the right neighborhood. My room was every little girl's dream—it even had a fireplace. But that disappeared when I was twelve—my mom and dad divorced. We went from having everything to sporting a big black X on our backs—or so it seemed. The shame I felt was overwhelming. Time passed, but the childhood wounds just scabbed over.

Then I meet my first husband. He was my knight in shining armor, my everything. He was everything right. But I discovered he was a con man. The charmed life I was living was all a sham. When he was sent to prison, I felt shame. And old sores reopened and seeped. My belief system shattered. If I made wrong choices, who can I trust?

By the time I meet and marry Bob, who is the provider extraordinaire, I was riddled with guilt and shame. I felt worthless. Bob saw a different woman than the one I saw in the mirror. I woke up every morning feeling heavy—buried in shame. I was anxious about everything, even though I didn't have a solid reason. My bags were so heavy, I needed someone to help me unpack. It was the beginning of getting rid of the past.

Finding My Purpose to Heal

Alice and I spend two and half hours together on the first day. After she finished her humming thing with me, we sit down and start talking. She asked question after question. As we talked,

I took notes. It still amazes me that the very first thing in my notebook reads, "Thoughts and emotions create how we feel; our energy creates our health or disease." I was no stranger to that idea, but I'd never looked at it so carefully. Wow! Talk about taking responsibility — and to be honest, it was a little hard to confront at first. All the shame and anxiety I carried every day was creating energy that was creating the disease in my body.

Remember how I would conjure up other people's diseases as my own? That fact hit me like five tons of bricks. Alice said, "Thought is the core. Where you are putting your intention becomes a model of experience about to happen. If your thoughts tend in the direction of worry or fear" — how does she know that about me? — "then that's what you get." If my thoughts created how I felt, and my intentions created the experience that was about to happen, if I concentrated on worry and fear all the time…well, it was staring me plain in the face: *I did this to myself.*

Alice didn't let me chew on that one for very long, thank goodness. I could have beaten myself up about it. Instead, she quickly led me down a path that put all that shame and anxiety in its place. She said, "There are techniques for manifestation." I knew about affirmations — who doesn't? — but I didn't understand how they work. Alice said, "Affirmations are putting out to the universe what you desire to be in terms of what you *are.*" She then gave me a quick list of other techniques. She started with the affirmations "I am peace! I am serenity." Then she told me that every day I had to *thank God* (I double underlined that in my notes) for what *is* before it happens, to acknowledge that something is occurring even before it happens in the physical universe. I thought that was some heavy stuff, but it beat the way I dealt with the past.

Alice said I needed to practice visualization ("a picture is worth a thousand words," I wrote in my book) and feel the feelings I wanted to have. That one threw me a bit. I wasn't good at feeling, but Alice told me I needed to be willing to experience any feeling. I needed to go into my mind and into my body to feel what it's like to have health. I needed to create what I wanted to have happen.

Above all, I needed to have faith that the process works. I had to find it in myself to believe that I could heal myself. I needed to learn how to become what I wanted — and to do that, I had to name what I wanted. I immediately knew the answer to that one: I wanted to feel light, to love, to laugh, to sing, and to be joyful. I wanted to manifest every day a high-vibration energy, because as Alice explained, if you're sad, you attract sadness. If you're joyful, you attract joy. What a concept!

She asked me to list everything I wanted to be and feel. I needed to find my purpose, to see what my next steps would look like and feel like. As we talked, I wrote,

> I am healthy and free! I am strong, in shape, and helping others.
>
> Thank you, God, for allowing my studio to grow so that I can help so many people.
>
> I see myself as a fun-loving, young Mimi [grand-mother], enjoying my grandbabies, swimming in the surf, and giving them lots of love.
>
> I see myself as the next Lotte Burke [the woman who created one of the most effective exercise programs fifty years ago], flourishing in my business and being successful.
>
> My marriage is full of joy and love.
>
> I see myself doing some things with my mom, writing a book together and joining forces.
>
> My purpose is to nurture and encourage people to take care of themselves. I want to share my mission.
>
> I start my days joyful, grateful, and thankful. Thank you, God, for this today and every day. Thank you,

God, for my health and my freedom. I am at peace.
I already am

It's interesting that I didn't finish the last sentence, either with a word or with a period. It left a place for what I could create in the future, which meant that I *have* a future. It was the first time since I heard the news that I had cancer that I was certain of that thought. For the first time in a long time, I started to feel lighter and freer. It was delicious! I had been depriving myself; to even taste it was like sweet nectar.

Alice ended our first session by telling me what we were going to do. She was going to help me find mastery, to learn to live in the present, to learn to reset with the new moon. She said, "We're going to do an alignment with our soul." And then she gave me what I have always considered a poem:

Soul conceives

Mind creates

Body experiences

Conception should come from the soul.

Use my mind as a tool

Experience we have grown we miss the first step by going to ego first.

We are going to the heart

Wisdom, guidance, and knowing is in your heart.

Her closing words to me were that I needed to do some homework. I needed to draw a picture that represented what I wanted to have happen. "Images have enormous power," she said, and I knew exactly what I would draw — a water lily, because no matter what the condition of the water, they bloom. Inside the center petal would be a peace sign, because I knew that I needed to find peace inside me. And sitting on the petal would be a butterfly — the ultimate symbol of transformation.

As I left I sensed that all I had done up to that moment had been just preliminary. This was going to be the real work, the stuff that added the umph to the Reiki, the acupuncture, and especially those *nasty* herbs. (I never did get used to the taste, by the way. I just got use to drinking them.) I make Alice a once-a-week priority, as important as my herbs, my acupuncture, and my chi walking—and boy, was I in for it. (More about the chi walking later.)

Learning to Let Go

The work with Alice wasn't easy, especially when we first started. Sometimes I wanted to cancel. I tried to create excuses, because it was hard and exhausting. It was all hard—the herbs, the acupuncture, everything—but the more I did it, the more it made sense to me. Did anything I was doing make sense to anyone else? Probably not, but the more work I did, the more I didn't care. If I thought someone was saying things behind my back, "Poor thing. She's avoiding what's really to come," I'd think, *Well, if I can avoid it a little longer, I'm okay with that.*

After that first session with Alice, I realized that I needed to let go of a lot—anger, frustration, all the negative emotions. I believed it kept the cancer inside my body.

I knew that conventional therapy didn't work. I had tried that, both by myself and with Bob. Mom had told me for years that therapy would help my anxiety. When I did go, I told the therapist that I needed some assurance that I wasn't crazy, that I wasn't making stuff up. I felt all we did was have me cry, "Wah wah wah." With Bob, it always would come down to who was going to be the most right. Therapy seemed to keep going over and over the surface; it didn't get to the deep stuff.

The next time Alice and I met, we dived down deep. I don't remember exactly what Alice asked me, but I remember the answer. Ever since my mom and dad divorced, back in the early seventies, I'd felt abandoned—by my mother and later by my ex-husband, Jake. I was also incredibly angry at Jake. When he was around—which wasn't often—I felt like I was going insane.

While there were many issues to confront, Alice and I decided to start with my Jake, because he wasn't in the picture anymore, so he was, in some ways, easier to confront. We dived in.

A Story of Insanity

I met Jake when I was nineteen. I'd spent my teenage years as a rebel. I was mad at my parents for disrupting my life and sending me away to live with my crazy grandmother. When I returned from my year at Grannie's, I was even more sullen and difficult. I hung out with a tough crowd, started smoking, and got into enough trouble to drive my mother crazy. She sent me away to boarding school.

When I hit puberty, I went from being a stick figure to having a curvy, semi-voluptuous look. And I was torn. I wasn't nurtured by my dad as a girl; I was treated like a boy. He wanted me to be tough, not prissy, so I acted like a tomboy. When I got my curves, I also wanted to be sexy. When I got to boarding school, I began to fall apart emotionally. My mother never seemed to have time to visit me. My grandmother came on some weekends, but I don't know if that was a blessing or a curse. I started closet eating to compensate for my loneliness. Something was missing, but I wasn't sure what or why.

I " blew up" to 165 pounds. I went from a cute tomboy blonde to a chubby girl.

So many women have image issues, and we stuff so much angst, anger, and God-knows-what into our bodies in the form of food. I certainly was stuffing my feelings. I was miserable and unhappy. Food was my comfort. The bingeing was madness; it made me miserable. It also had a spiraling effect. Eating was satisfying in the moment of numbing, but the repercussions were heavy. I adopted another compulsive behavior: I ate and then exercised all day. I was considered a pretty girl by my peers, but eating changed that all for me. Kids called me "fat ass," and it hurt me to the core. I tried so hard to diet, but my compulsive personality engaged in an all-or-nothing battle with my body. I overate and then worked out three hours a day to burn the calories. I was only able to maintain my weight.

When I met Jake, I was ready to be swept off my feet. He was charming. He said all the right things. He could have any woman, and I was thrilled that he chose me. He made me feel like a princess. I was at my all-time heaviest, and he still wanted me.

We met when Jake came into the magazine company I was working for out on Long Island. It's a well-known place called Dan Rattiner. I was the clerk behind this huge counter, and I was also Dan's nanny to his young children for the summer. I believe the counter was the key. Jake could see me only from the chest up, and I had all the goods there. We'd chitchat, and I'd think nothing of it until I saw him again at the post office. He asked me out to lunch and the rest, as they say, is history.

Jake always managed to say the right things and to treat me so lovingly. He was poetic, nurturing, and wanted to take care of me. I think I want to be taken care of so, it was a perfect fit. Little did I know the hidden price attached.

Jake slowly seduced me into his web of lies and deceit. He created a different web than the one Grannie was weaving—and she was the master. I believed in my heart Jake loved me; he just didn't believe in following rules. That would be fine if he were out on an island, but in reality, everyone needs to follow the law. It's there for a reason.

From the very beginning, Jake made me feel like a princess—something I never had from any man—and it was intoxicating. He was giving me everything my parents wouldn't or couldn't. He acknowledged me when I needed it. He said what I needed to hear. Before meeting Jake, I felt like a burden to everyone. This "love" I felt helped me lose the weight. Food became a choice, not an escape. I was full because Jake loved and wanted me. But it came at a cost.

Jake was not only charming, he was a genius—he scored a perfect score on his SATs. He came from what looked like a solid family—parents still married, two sisters, and all living in their happy, fairytale world on an estate complete with horses. While I love all animals, horses have a special place in my universe. Jake and his mother ran the horse farm on their estate, and when Jake found out how much I knew about horses, he invited me to live on the estate and take care of them. As a carrot, he threw in a Porsche. How could any girl resist that?

But Jake had a problem. He was all over the place—literally, he didn't know if he was coming or going, inside or outside. It was a constant roller coaster of "I'm coming," "I'm going," "I'm leaving," "I'm staying." It was hard for him to be precise. This was crazy, but after all those years with Grannie, I was used to all kinds of crazy. I could flow with it. It was familiar to me.

When I met Jake, I was emotionally raw. Somewhere deep down I knew he wasn't right for me. But I ignored my heart, quieted my inner voice, and rationalized away all the inconsistencies. If I caught him in a lie, he lavished me with gifts. If I caught him smoking pot, I just left. I started stuffing down all the hurt I felt, deep into my heart. Most of the time he gave me so much of what I thought I wanted.

It took my work with Alice to recognize that I wanted to fix him and make him right. I still work on this behavior. It's not an easy one. I want to be helped, and I struggle every day with myself wanting to help people who just don't care. I want to do the right thing and be the best I can—but before I found how to balance that desire with letting go of what couldn't be, it was utterly exhausting.

I believe in my heart that Jake loved me. Early on, he provided some sense of normalcy for me. After all, he lived on the farm I'd always dreamed of. It was comfort on a grand scale—the family compound and the restored barns-turned-lofts. Our home was the upper part of an old potato barn. It was really neat. We could see all the pastures from our decks, along with the horses. I was in heaven.

Then it started to unravel. Yes, Jake could do extraordinary things. One time he sold a horse for 450,000 dollars. But he would not live under normal rules—he needed constant drama. In hindsight, I believe he was the definition of a sociopath, lying and scheming at every turn.

We hadn't been together very long when he gave me a horse for my birthday. The horse was named Jake. Horse Jake became not just my horse but also my best friend and confidant. This beautiful animal was one of the bright spots in my world, especially when my world went dark. He was a beautiful Dutch Warmblood imported from Europe, feisty and full of pride. Jake's value increased as I worked with him and trained him for hours. He was everything to me — the constant companion I loved for years.

A neighbor of ours liked him and wanted to have part ownership in him. Husband Jake, being perennially short of cash, decided to sell half my horse. This wasn't an unusual occurrence, as there are many racehorses that have partial owners. But Jake was my horse — not his to sell. The next problem surfaces when I found out that Jake had leveraged my horse against a piece of property that he was selling to the neighbor. So my "birthday present" became security for a piece of land. Jake was working to sell subdivided plots of this land before he went through all the legalities. He skirted the law whenever he could, I found out later. What angered me the most was that he used my horse to secure the deal. The neighbor bought half my horse for a paltry ten thousand dollars. Eventually, the land deal fell apart because it isn't legal. By that time, the property already had several mortgages, and the neighbor wanted my animal as payment for the collateral she'd advanced.

When Jake told me, I was devastated. *How can this possibly happen?* I thought. I act quickly — my misspent youth had taught me to be tough and think on my feet. I called a shipping company specifically for horses and shipped my horse to Massachusetts. By that time, we had our first child, Tyler, and I was scared. I was beginning to see a pattern. Jake would give me something, but then because of his schemes and such, someone would take it away. I was beginning to fear for my son. If Jake was so willing to take my horse, what would he do with my son?

The main issue was money. His mother doted on him. She bailed him out time and time again, but I wasn't about to start that pattern. Once I figured out that the property was an estate, I didn't want Jake to squander away the remaining funds. As time wore on, I watched Jake abuse his mother's legacy, along with her soul. She so loved her son. But I felt she knew there was something fundamentally not right about him. He would lie and create stories that sounded believable. He was so convincing, I doubted my sanity at times, but eventually the stories spiraled out of control. He made up stories about drugs, about everything. I couldn't trust him, but I was broken and willing to put up with his behavior. I begged him to just lead a normal life. I asked him why he needed drama. Giving me a straight or true answer seemed like a foreign concept to him.

Then the final straw. Shortly after he tried to give my horse away, I found a bag of pot in Tyler's crib. I cringe when I think of what could have happened if Tyler found the bag. I had earlier found something Jake calls "horse pills" in his shoe while organizing his closet. I later found out they were quaaludes—a sedative that can also be used as a hypnotic. Jake was getting high all day long. I began to worry about our future, and old feelings of abandonment began to wrap around my heart like a kudzu vine.

We left Jake and the dream behind. Tyler was one. I rented a little house in the area. Life was simpler. Jake tried to get me to come back, but I was scared. I stayed away for five months but felt pressured to return. My mom told me Jake was a good man and I needed to give him a second chance. In a weird twist, the new Jake had snowed her too. Jake convinced me he was going to be good and everything was going to be fine. "I'm not doing drugs anymore," he promised. I caved. I went back to him, stupid me. I ignored the anger, pushing it deeper into the smoldering furnace.

Every weekend Jake went into the city on business. I found out later he was checking into his halfway house. This time it was no different. He was hiding what he was doing. But I still had a "savior complex"; I wanted to save him. When Tyler turned two, I got pregnant with Nick—by choice. I thought it would help make Jake a better parent, make him a better person. He ultimately ended up in jail.

He was also tied into the mafia. Turns out, Jake was spending his time in Manhattan working on some big deal, a limited partnership, by selling parts of the farm to investors. He was financing the whole deal through a loan shark. His loan was at 24 percent interest. What finally caught him was a twelve-million-dollar wire scam.

We were staying at the Helmsley Palace (now the New York Palace.) I was seven months pregnant, and the FBI showed up at our door. Fortunately, we were in the lobby. As the agents approached Jake, he said to me, "Don't worry. Go sit over there for a minute." The FBI didn't take him to jail that time.

When Nick was about nine months old, they brokered a plea bargain with Jake. He would go into protection and out others to the FBI. I didn't see him for months. I was terrified the whole time he was gone. I didn't know if I was going to be killed or if someone would come after me. Every time I got into my car, I held my breath, because I didn't know if it would blow up. Life was a living hell. I lived in fear. I couldn't continue.

I served Jake divorce papers while he was in jail. That's when the real games began. I've never understood it, but then again, insanity by definition is incomprehensible. Why wouldn't a person want to put his energies into just following the rules? Life is so much easier when you do that. Jake had never seen it that way. I had decided that I didn't want a life filled with the mafia or the FBI trailing our every step. I didn't know when he would be picked up for his next scam, and I wanted more than anything to protect my children. But Jake wasn't going to let me escape easily. He didn't like to lose—at anything. If he thought you were a challenge or that you were challenging him, he would try to outsmart you, and that's what he tried to do to me.

For the next twenty years, he waged an all-out war on my sanity. The only respite I got was when he was in jail. Even then, he sent me letters telling me that he had changed. He told me, "I have found God." He sent letters begging for my forgiveness. He swore he had learned his lesson. It all sounded good and convincing. I decided that he needed to participate in his sons' upbringing as much as he could. I sent him all the boys' homework. I had Ty and Nick write letters to him so that he could stay connected. But it was all another big lie on Jake's part — and a big mistake on mine.

Eventually, Jake started his scheming and scamming again, even in jail. The worry I felt was overwhelming. I became paranoid. I constantly felt like he was plotting to get back at me for taking his boys away from him. I was thirty-two when I started having frequent and severe panic attacks. I'd had them since I was a child, but they became more frequent and far more intense. At one point, I was convinced that Jake would arrange to have me killed so he could take the boys. It wasn't an idle threat or my being crazy. In his letters and phone calls, he made sure I knew how many ways he was capable of making that happen. This threat kept me from allowing the boys to visit him. And he never paid me a dime in child support.

When I met Bob, it got worse. I served Jake divorce papers in 1992 and married Bob in 1994. When Jake got out of prison, he started the process all over again. He moved to New York City and acquired the one-million-dollar art fortune his mom had left him. He seduced some unsuspecting woman, convincing her he had all this money, and then bilked her out of her fortune.

I was furious. He was living a lavish life, driving Jaguars and wearing expensive clothing. When I told him, "You need to pay child support," he said, "I don't have any money. It's my girlfriend's. She supports this lifestyle for me." Most of the time, this was true. He was brilliant at finding desperate, emotionally weak women — just like I was — that wanted to take care of him. He had a gift of convincing you that you wanted to hand everything over to him. Even as I write this, I still can't believe how many times he conned me. Looking back, I'm amazed at the enormous amount of blind trust I had in him.

I soon found it hard to trust anybody, even my wonderful new husband. To me, the saddest thing of all is that Jake's aberrant behavior created such disharmony in my relationship with Bob. It is amazing how Jake could create wars without even being there. Bob and I had some of our worst fights over Jake. Bob was trying to protect us all and provide us with a comfortable life while Jake was destroying our lives. I let the kids visit him on occasion. I still feel it was the right thing to do, letting them foster their own relationship. But that quickly turned ugly too.

Jake moved to Atlanta, right into our neighborhood. It gets worse. We lived in an exclusive, gated community. He was a master at pitting the boys against me, and I spent an inordinate amount of my day worrying over how to protect them. Then on the news one day, there was Jake, being walked out of the house by the FBI for some scam. I still don't know what that was all about; I probably never will, and that's okay.

I had another few years of respite after that. Things began to calm into a comfortable routine. But all good things must end, and we heard Jake was living in downtown Atlanta, in a gorgeous penthouse. At that point, Ty was almost fifteen. One day, I was driving downtown, and I looked to my right. To my horror, there was my son, driving a Jaguar—but he didn't even have a permit. I felt my heart race, and the anger began to bore even deeper into me.

It was the classic push-me-pull-me syndrome. I told my sons one thing, and Jake said the exact opposite. Jake told the boys that I was crazy, and sometimes it looked that way. I would get furious over something the boys did, but they would blithely tell me that "Dad said it was okay." Being thirteen and fourteen years old, they were going to play whatever side could benefit them the most.

We relocated to the beach to get away from Jake. He followed us. He showed up at Nick's baseball game. The worst part was that, no matter what else is going on, Jake gave the boys wads of one-hundred-dollar bills to win them over. He taught them how to be irresponsible and disrespectful. He told my sons that *everything* that ever happened to him was not his fault. "They are just out to get me," he would tell them. It led them to believe that they could do anything they wanted without any repercussions. But life choices are filled with consequences, both good and bad.

Releasing Anger

Before I was diagnosed with cancer, I tried to forgive myself for the terrible mistake of allowing this person to be a part of my life. I hated that I'd exposed my children to such a dysfunctional human being. Before I got sick, I believed the only way to make myself feel better was to fix everyone else.

I'm still amazed at how quickly the threat of death changes things. It was hard to tell my husband and my mother that I had cancer, but it was devastating to break the news of my disease to my boys. Tyler and Nick are my heart and soul. I have such unconditional love for them. Yes, I get angry with them, and they frustrate the hell out of me sometimes, but they're my children.

I told Nick first. He was a high school senior and definitely "the man": good looking and charming. He was also hanging out with the wrong crowd, which was hard for me to watch. I had made the same stupid mistakes when I was his age, and I knew his rebellion had to do with the weird dynamics between Jake and me. It's true that the kids get the fallout when we fight.

Nick was getting ready for prom when I decided to tell him, But I waited. I remember him coming home after the prom and me still wondering how I would tell him. I'd tried for so long to protect him from all evil—especially his father—and now…I can't even finish the thought.

When I heard Nick come in, I said, "Son, you need to come upstairs to my room." I'm sure I looked like hell. I had been sobbing all afternoon at the thought of leaving my babies. Now I had to share my deepest worst fears. When I told him, his eyes welled up, and he looked at me with disbelief. (Maybe that is the standard response when you tell people such news. It helped me not to be so angry at my husband for having the same reaction.)

It felt like some sick soap opera. "Well, son, not only has your biological father abandoned you, but I'm checking out sooner than later as well." I told him that he had a good support system in place. I told him, "It's time for you to step up to the plate and start acting right." He knew what I meant by that. He also knew that I was always trying to protect him and his brother, whether it was from my ex or from their own foolishness. I was a constant policewoman, pacing back and forth, waiting for them to do something stupid. I told him I couldn't do that anymore.

Bless his heart. My Nick stepped up to the plate and showed me that he could make better choices and not be so foolish. He has come a long way and is now in his second year of college. I'm so proud of what a stellar young man he is becoming.

Tyler was away at college, so I called him with the news. I think that I probably damaged him for life. You know what they say about the firstborn child. We usually wreck them with our neurotic behavior. Tyler has the toughest deal of all, because he's older than Nick and bore the brunt of all the mixed messages. He used to never call unless he needed something, or I called him. He started calling me every day. He would infuse me with loving and powerful messages. He started becoming more expressive and letting me know more and more how much he loves me. He also made more of an effort to come and visit.

Tyler is my calm energy with a brilliant mind. He let me know he would watch over his baby brother and guide him through the good and bad times. I will say I've been given one gift: my boys truly love each other. They're so different, but they have a deep connection through all the madness that has gone on.

Best of all, they have proven Grannie wrong. She always told me that one decision could ruin the rest of my life. My boys are living proof that she was off-base on that one. We all make decisions, good and bad, but it's up to us to take responsibility for those decisions and move on with our lives. Yes, I made the decision to marry and have a family with Jake. Yes, he is who he is, but I have to come to terms with the fact that I was allowing him to make my life miserable. I'm the one who was constantly upset over what he was doing to my boys.

With Alice's help, I was able to let go of that anger. I recognized that I was constantly watching my children—so much that I never got a chance to relax. I was in a chronic state of stress, but I didn't realize it because I was too busy trying to protect my kids from Jake's behavior, his mixed messages, his destruction.

It was so freeing to start releasing the toxins that had built up from all that anger and anxiety. I only feel safe when he's behind bars—and that's where we believe he is. None of us has heard from him since I was diagnosed. When I released the anger I felt toward him, I broke the bond that connected us. It's interesting— when you handle things in your own universe, other people get the vibe or something and shift their behavior as well.

All I can say is, I'm glad my boys are now grown. They know the score, and it's up to them to decide if they want a relationship with their father. I'm sure Jake will still try to grovel himself into their lives and try to convince them he's a changed man. He will tell them, "I'm not willing to pay your mother for all the years of back child support," but he'll try to buy their love. I'm sure he won't try to contact me, because I'll work to have him pay all the back child support he owes me. I do my best to give my boys the best messages about responsibility and doing the right things.

Learning to let go is a gift in itself. Letting go helps me breathe. Cancer gave me the gift of being able to say, "It's now out of my hands." I pray the Serenity Prayer every day, and I believe what I say:

God grant me the serenity to accept the things I cannot change;

courage to change the things I can;

and wisdom to know the difference.

Living one day at a time;

Enjoying one moment at a time;

Accepting hardships as the pathway to peace;

Taking, as He did, this sinful world as it is, not as I would have it;

Trusting that He will make all things right if I surrender to His Will;

That I may be reasonably happy in this life and supremely happy with Him Forever in the next.

Amen.

—Reinhold Niebuhr

Forgiveness
CHAPTER 6

Learning How to Forgive

It's amazing what happened once I started taking responsibility for those things that happened to me. When I started letting go of the anger I felt toward my ex-husband, I realized that my being a "victim" wasn't accomplishing anything except stressing me out. The stress and anger were making me sick.

Once I let go of that baggage, all sorts of interesting things start to happen. There is an old Buddhist saying, "When the student is ready, the master appears." In my case, the master is, the right therapy .

About a month into my first three months of watchful waiting, my Reiki instructor, Janet, asked me, "How do you feel about my doing a little unwinding?"

I had no idea what unwinding is. I knew about clocking—that's a basic Pilates exercise that has you moving your pelvis with your abs. I asked her if it is similar. "No, unwinding is actually called myofascial unwinding. It's a form of soft-tissue therapy intended for pain relief as well as increasing range of motion and balancing the body." The first time we did it, nothing happened in the cancer areas, but boy, did I feel a difference in my neck! I had an old neck injury from a severe car accident. Whether it was constant headaches or a stiff neck and range-of-motion issues, I lived with chronic pain. After that first unwinding session, I felt better and continued to feel better every time Janet treated that area.

Myofascial unwinding has another more interesting purpose. It was developed by a physical therapist named John F. Barnes. It's the most wonderful thing. Again, fascia is the connective tissue in the body. It surrounds every organ and connects everything in its web. When you're injured, the fascia helps create an environment for tissue repair. And get this: fascia plays an essential role in hemodynamic biochemical processes — that's a fancy way of saying it's essential in blood flow and every other chemical process that happens in your body, *and* it provides the medium that allows for intercellular communication.

Considering I have cancer of the blood and lymph, and cancer is a disease of cells gone wild, this was all very intriguing to me. I thought my fascia needed as much help and attention as I could give it. *Unwind away!* Janet told me that all I needed to do was relax. I was getting better at that, and at least the unwinding wouldn't cause any pain. She then explained the procedure in more depth. The therapist's job is to remove gravity from whatever is being worked on. For instance, she may lift a patient's arm and just support it, allowing natural movement of the body to occur. The movement may begin with the arm and may move to other parts or the whole body. It can be free flowing or very intense. Through the tissue's changing tensions, the body produces a motion that is followed, not led, by the therapist's sensitive hands. This amazing process enables a gradual release of fascia restrictions.

Okay, that's good stuff, I thought, but then it got really good. "Emotions or memories, called state- or position-dependent memories, can resurface when the body attains a position which it was in during a time of trauma," she said. Whoa. I was releasing a hell of a lot of emotion in my work with Alice. I wondered if this would facilitate matters.

She continued. "These significant positions cause a calming of the craniosacral rhythm to a still point." I didn't know what that meant, but it sounded good—and I didn't want to interrupt. Janet then delivered the goods: "Myofascial unwinding can eliminate fascia pressure from nerves and other structures resulting in elimination of pain and improved range of motion. Enabling this movement of the patient, but not forcing it, is unique to this type of therapy. It's neither invasive nor aggressive and is safe because the body doesn't do anything that would injure itself. Once the patient feels comfortable letting go during this process, the body-mind is capable of healing in quantum leaps."

There it was. I definitely needed healing in quantum leaps.

Myofascial unwinding is hard to describe, really. It feels as though the therapist is moving your body, when the movement is really coming from you. I loved getting it, and I don't know for a scientific fact if it made my work with Alice progress faster. But as I started unwinding my fascia, the web of anguish and abandonment I'd felt trapped in practically my entire life began to unwind as well.

Coming to Terms with Grannie

Though I was a misguided youth, I had what outsiders might consider a perfect childhood—that is, until I was twelve. My dad had a good job, and we lived in an upper-middle-class neighborhood. I had everything I could ever want. But on the inside, it wasn't so pretty. My mom and dad fought constantly. My mom, being a child of the fifties, was raised to be the perfect wife. I'm sure she hated it. She also had a terrible childhood. Her parents divorced when she was young, and then her mother, who was the ultra-controlling type, remarried—and the stepfather was an abusive nightmare.

In the early seventies, Mom basically kicked Dad out of the house. But it was the 1970s, and Mom, who has gone to college, needed to build up her career. Like so many other kids, my two brothers and I turned into latch-key kids. We had the run of the house until Mom got home. Being a twelve-year-old, I thought this is great. But, boy, can three preteen kids get into a lot of trouble.

After Dad left, I started hanging around a tougher crowd. My old friends rejected me. I was a pariah because my parents are "divorced," like somehow that made me dirty. I felt hugely ashamed, which I didn't understand at all, because it wasn't my fault that my parents couldn't get along with each other. I was at that point in my life when fitting in was top priority. Going to the tough crowd was the perfect solution at that point. My neighborhood seemed to have more than its fair share of bullies, so I had learned to be tough to survive.

Then when my parents split, I formed a Teflon layer to protect myself. Deep down, I was like any girl, a sensitive flower wanting to be loved. I wanted to be the princess I never was, and I needed layers of protection. I was bitter, angry, looking to be heard. Nobody would listen, except the wrong crowd. Everyone there was pretty much like me. Besides, they were cool, and if I was part of that crowd, I would be cool too. I desperately needed validation. I even started smoking right away. But what was I doing to my body?

That summer I went to visit Grannie. It was business as usual that summer — a lot of work, not much vacation. When I got home, I was beyond shocked. Mom had rented my room out to a boarder. My beautiful antique dollhouse was gone. I had spent hours playing with that house; I don't know how many times I changed the wallpaper. It had two antique dolls, and I loved playing make-believe with them. My mom said she got rid of it because she thought I was done with it. But I had dreamed of giving it to my little girl when I got to be a mommy.

My mother also got rid of my pet goose; to this day I suspect she cooked him. I was an animal fanatic. Before things fell apart, I had quite the menagerie: two beautiful white doves; Oscar, my goose; and even a couple of show chickens. Oscar was amazing. He walked me to the bus every day and picked me up after school. Really, he would come running to meet me at the bus stop. He was more than my pet; he was my protector. That same year, my beloved pony got hit by a car, and I held him as he died in my arms. The sadness I felt sank into my bones and into my heart.

My world was turned upside down. It took my work with Alice to understand how abandoned I felt. At thirteen, I just started rebelling, getting into as much trouble as I could. Now that I'm older with teenage sons who had Mr. Con Man for a dad, I can empathize with my mother. I'm sure I was more than just a handful, and I'm sure she didn't get rid of my goose or my doll-house with any intention to harm me. But it deeply saddened me, and I started to get angry at her. As a child I didn't know how to deal with everything that was going on inside me. I didn't want anything to do with my mother or my father, and the only solace I found was in my tough group of friends.

What was my mother to do? I was practically uncontrollable. She was just beginning her career, and she had to concentrate on making sure we had a roof over our heads. Grannie said, "Have Laurie come stay with me." So the process began. I was shipped off to Grannie's. Of course, everything was always done for "my benefit." I had to go to Grannie's because she'd bought a house in the Hamptons by a good school. This was probably a very good thing for me, but it made me mad because my brother Eric, the baby, got to stay with Mom.

I went to live with Grannie-dearest, and things got weird. My grandmother was a hard woman, as they say in the South. Living with her and the woman she raised, my mother, made me feel like I wasn't worthy of anything. I never felt I deserved good things to happen to me. As I watched and listened to my grandmother all those years, I began to believe that something bad would eventually happen to me. Those were my thoughts as a young child. Today I'm fully responsible for them, but it took a lot of unwinding—both emotionally and physically—to find out how deeply Grannie affected me.

Grannie loved me deeply. I knew that. She was always rescuing me from bad situations. She adored me the best she could, but she had a very bad habit of triangulating everyone around her. She pit me against my mother, my mother against me. She was constantly talking down about one person of the family to another. It was very hard and very confusing for me. Here was a woman who showed me that she loved me. At that point, I felt that Mom said all the right things, but then wouldn't back it up with action. The messages were mixed and fragile.

My grandmother was a very complex and disturbed woman. She came over on the boat from Italy when she was a young girl of nine; she spoke no English. She was one of five children, and at the age of five, she watched her three-year-old sister get killed right before her eyes. It was a subject we never talked about. I heard it from my mother years later. I guess Grannie was in charge of holding her sister's hand while crossing the street. Marie pulled away, fell off the curb, and was hit by a car. I believe this haunted Grannie all her life.

Grannie became the caretaker of her whole family as an older adult. Loretta, my mother, was abandoned by her mother to her mother's career. Grannie worked on Wall Street as a paralegal in some bigwig's office. Little Loretta was left at home with her grandmother. She eventually bought a brownstone in the Bronx. Every family member lived in the house, including her brothers. Shortly after everyone moved in, my mother's father, Lorenzo, contracted tuberculosis and was banned from the house; Grannie didn't want Mom exposed to this potentially fatal disease. After he left, Grannie found out Lorenzo was also having an affair, and this just made her bitter toward life.

Grannie married her second husband, Mario, who was considered a family friend and someone she thought could help her raise Loretta. Their marriage was not perfect. As time went on, their friendship shifted into deep resentment toward each other. Grandmother constantly berated grandfather. They would have horrible fights right in front of Mom, throwing pots and pans at each other. As an adult, I had to acknowledge the inherent patterns that were all too apparent. Mom was abandoned by her first dad, who started a whole new family and left my Mom behind. She then was raised by a crazy stepfather who hated her mother and abused her. This would not foster strong emotional stability in anyone.

The only real stability Loretta had was with her grandmother, whom they called Little Grandma, but she was out of the picture by the time Loretta was ten. My mother told me that she has never felt safe since then. Her mother, Laura, was still the primary breadwinner. She left her job as a paralegal and became successful in the real-estate business. And like me, Loretta resented the hell out of that. She wanted her mother, not some well-off career woman. To make matters worse, Grannie could be relentless. She was a total "Mommy Dearest" type of control freak. This was the woman that I was sent to live with after my parents divorced.

It was made even more complicated because I always looked at Grannie as my saving grace, and even though I didn't like that I had to work all summer long, I loved going to her house when I was little. She was my safe haven, or so I thought. While she always did come to my rescue, I learned later that there was always some price attached — just like Jake.

It was such a bag of mixed messages. My dad didn't get along at all with Grannie, although I suspect he admired her work ethic. My mom couldn't stand to be around her. When we were at Grannie's for the summer, we never saw our mother. To me, at least Grannie wanted to be with me and be a part of my life, unlike my mom, who was always caught up in her busy life.

But all was not as it appeared. Grannie's crazy making happened behind my back. While she would be doing all these wonderful things for me, she would be bitching about it to everyone else. The target of her vitriol never knew this. I only realized it later, when Alice and I did our work. I started looking at all that happened when Grannie came to live with me.

Grannie made her gossiping seem like it was a good thing; you were in a conspiracy against the other person. She would say, "Now, don't tell your mother I just let you know this." Ooh, I had dirt on my mom, and since I was liking her less and less, that made me feel special. But Grannie's admonition to secrecy was giving me negative messages about someone else. Since I wasn't supposed to say anything about it to anyone else, I had to stuff the secrets deep down inside.

It didn't stop there. Grannie would gossip about a family member but, when she was around them, she would act so differently that it made me think that what she said was a lie. Who knew what was real and what was a lie? Grannie became more conniving the older she got. I felt like I was in some psychotic movie. I questioned my own sanity. I didn't know what was true. This created an unhealthy triangular relationship among Mom, me, and Grannie. Grannie would talk bad about her daughter, and since my Mom grew up with Grannie, she would talk bad about Grannie. The dysfunctional pattern was being passed down to the next generation: Grannie talked bad about me to Mom and then denied it, and then did the same with me about my mother.

Walking My Way to Health

It's no wonder I became sick. I had so much resentment and anger built up inside of me. I was trying so hard to be the perfect wife to Bob, the perfect mother to my children, the perfect everything to everyone. I stuffed all this poison down inside me. It's funny in a way. I had spent countless hours, weeks, months, even years, trying to fix everyone else. I didn't know how to fix me, and I'm sure I was trying to fix others in an attempt to heal my heart. I didn't know how to let any of it out in any safe ways until I met Alice. With her, week after week, we would go through more. She just listened, asking the occasional question. She was wonderful in that she let me figure it out; her job was simply to help me open up. And it was coming out in buckets.

I had started to develop a routine—herbs, food, acupuncture, healing work. I also added chi walking. I read about it in one of the books someone sent (probably Mom), and I adopted it in light of the "what do I have to lose" refrain. I love walking and have walked for exercise all my life. But it was all about the exercise. It was time I put on headphones and did some serious walking.

With chi walking, I learned what walking is really all about. It's more about the experience than the exercise. It's about the positive messages I play over and over in my mind. I pay attention to thinking about every breath I take with each step. Instead of shutting out the world, I let it in. I love hearing the birds, and since I live by the Gulf of Mexico, I walk on the beach and delight in the rhythm of the waves. Through chi walking, I also I learned to feel the energy of the earth. It has become more of a meditative walk, and it's something I do religiously, every day.

I worked my routine daily. I woke up and took a mental tour through my body. I paid attention to each organ, especially the sick ones, and sent them all a lot of love. I learned to listen to what was going on—and there was a lot going on. The herbs were working their magic—and in very visible ways. I had canker sores on my mouth and other rashes coming and going all the time. Sometimes I felt my spleen and it was getting bigger, and sometimes the swelling abated.

At first it worried the hell out of me. *Am I getting better? Worse?* I couldn't tell. I'd wake Bob up in the middle of the night, and he'd just listen as he held me. I was letting go of so many buried, negative emotions, I cried. He cried with me. (And he's not one to cry. He probably learned early on that crying was for sissies. He's also an ex-football player and is not a wimp by any stretch of the imagination.) He knew, somehow, that the best thing he could do at that point was listen. He couldn't fix me. I think he figured that out early on. This was my battle. He had to let me fight it. The best thing he could do was just be there when I needed him—to listen, to hold me, to remind me that I was a strong woman full of life, to give me constant assurance that I could and would beat this thing. He became, truly, my knight in shining armor, not because he rescued me, but because he did what he did. He loved me throughout the ordeal.

Healing is a very up and down process; there are good days and bad days. The alternative route I chose wasn't an easy path. It was painful and uncomfortable; uncertainty was always biting at my heels. While Bob became my rock, walking was my solace. Every day, I went out for at least an hour and took Dixie with me. Dixie is my girl, a Jack Russell. Dogs are amazing beings. They know when we're sick. I'll never forget while my spleen

Love from Emeril

Mom and Me on the
Coast of California

Dad and Me on the
back deck at my home

All my sweet children-a wonderful day at the beach

Grannie

Bob's favorite girls:
Laurie(me), Mama D(Bob's Mom)
and Melissa (daughter).

*My horse training days with
my best friend's daughter, Ashley*

*My dear horse Jeff
and son Tyler age ?*

*Bob and I
living our dream.*

*Bob feeling not just the love..
but the wine!*

Bob's second love-Football.

was bulging out of my belly, she wanted to lie right there. She never missed a day of making sure she was supporting me. She also knew when it is walk time. We did our chi walk, and this was our time to work on my lymphatic system. She watched me intently as I said my affirmations out loud.

Part of Alice's homework assignments were affirmations — positive self-talk. I'd say them religiously. "I am healthy. I am alive. My organs are healing and becoming strong." It was a litany of positive energy. I infused my body with positive words. In fact, Alice taught me how to be positive. From the minute my eyes open, I infused every positive thought imaginable. "Thank you for this day, thank you for my health, thank you for my family, friends, dogs, the sun, the moon, and my ongoing healing journey." Whatever good I thought of, I said.

I was sometimes put to the test when it came to remaining positive. One beautiful day I was out walking. Instead of going to the beach, I went toward town. This took me past one of my neighbors, who is a doctor. Whenever he saw me, he stopped me. He asked the usual "How are you" questions.

I said I was doing great, even though I wasn't.

He said, "You look great for being so sick."

I thought, *What the hell does that mean?* Then he proceeded to tell me horror stories of people who just recently died of cancer.

I was thinking, *Are you serious?* Now, I always try to keep my composure and smile, but that day was different.

He told me, "Laurie, you are amazing. I have had patients die on the table with your white cell count."

I smiled. I knew he meant well, and I wished I could have gently told him that his words weren't helpful, no matter how well meaning they were. I look at him and thought, *Who is benefiting from this?* And I walked away, vowing never to walk past his house again.

I stuck mainly to the beach. It was soothing, and I need that, because I felt lousy much of the time. I was experiencing something called a healing crisis, which is when one feels worse before feeling better. It was scary, so my walks by the ocean were more than important; they were vital. They were the times I set aside during the day to inject all good into my body. I walked the beach and created a rhythm with the water. As the waves came in, I infused good energy from Mother Nature. I felt the energy of that wave flush out my body, and then as the water went out, it pulled out the bad cells. I was washing all sickness away.

The first three months of watchful waiting were up. It was time go to the doctor.

Finding Peace with Grannie

As I was getting ready for my second trip to Boston, I decided that, after the work I had done with Alice, it would be good to visit Grannie. At that point, I didn't know if I was going to live or not. I did love her, warts and all, and I wanted to at least say good-bye. For three years Grannie had lived in the nursing home. Her memory was pretty much shot, so I didn't know what to expect. We had departed on such painful terms. As I prepared for whatever was to come, I thought of all the ironies. I was fighting for my life, and she was living in a place she had feared her entire life. Neither of us was in the place we thought we'd be.

I also felt deeply the sorrow that she must have carried her whole life. We both were in such darkness for most of our lives. I was glad that I was starting to see the light. I was so emotionally torn. There I was, going back to the doctors, and I might hear potentially more devastating news. Though my desire was to go visit Grannie, I still had unresolved issues.

One of the greatest gifts I've received in this healing journey is learning how powerful it is to forgive. Whatever I did in my work with Alice had the most unexpected result. When Grannie saw me, she was delighted. Then she started to sob. She kept telling me how sorry she was for all that she had done. "Laurie, I was so wrong for what I did, and for what I said. I hope you'll forgive me."

I was astounded. Here was a woman who had severe dementia, a woman who remembered very little and didn't recognize me when I first walked into her room. But she remembered what happened. She kept repeating her words. Then she started pulling at my heartstrings and begging me to take her home. I was balling my eyes out; I had all these mixed emotions. I wanted to take her, to fulfill my promise to her. I also knew that she had a lot of her own demons. She didn't know I was sick. She never knew, because I chose not to tell her.

I had to make a hard decision. I remembered what I had told my family three months prior — that it was now "me" time. I had to honor that. When I make a promise, I damn sure keep it. But I couldn't with Grannie. I tried to explain to her that I couldn't take her home, because she wasn't strong enough. She needed skilled nursing and around-the-clock care. What I didn't have the heart to tell her was that I had moved on in my life. She was a very sick person, mentally and physically, and I didn't want that back in my life, even if I were healthy.

She is hanging onto me, and I had to control my feelings. I finally said, "I have to go to an appointment. I love you, Grannie, and I forgive you. I'll be back to see you." When I let her know she was forgiven, I truly feel it in my heart. Ironically, I thanked Alice felt in that moment, because I knew that if I hadn't let go of the past hurts in our work together, I would never have been able to have that moment of pure forgiveness.

Then something even more unbelievable happened. I had carried around me a deep, dark energy that was connected to my grandmother. It had invaded my body years earlier and haunted me my whole life. As I forgave her, that nasty energy instantly left. I felt a huge weight lift off of me. Everything was brighter — it even felt like my breath was more powerful — cleaner somehow. It was amazing.

When we hugged each other good-bye, I gave her every ounce of my love and thanked her for being my grandmother. Tears welled up in my eyes, knowing we could never go back in time. As I looked at her, so old and frail, I decided to remember the Grannie that I loved. I put all my happy memories of her in one loving compartment so that I could infuse those thoughts throughout my body and hers.

I went back to see Grannie. Before she died, she barely recognized me and didn't remember a thing. I remembered and inhaled the lightness of forgiveness. I think of the irony: the one thing that she fought her whole life was the place where she ended up. That's a life lesson for all of us.

The Real Power of Forgiveness

At that point in my healing journey, I didn't know what would happen. I affirmed life every day, but I didn't even know if I would have another birthday. But as I let go of the anger over my ex-husband and the resentment I had toward Grannie and Mom, I experienced the real power in forgiveness. Forgiveness is simply the power of letting go, of acknowledging "it is what it is." It doesn't absolve wrongdoing or the pain it caused. I let it go. I had a life-threatening force going on, so it wasn't worth the energy and effort to hang on to the anger, resentment, and hate. There is no payoff in being angry. It's a poison. I deal with my part, take responsibility, and after I make my peace with the past, I let it be just that, the past. Nothing matters at this point, except to be in a better place to heal and help others heal. To me, the real power of forgiveness is realizing that I am forgiving these people, not for their sake, but for mine. I want to live free. As Alice told me, the important part of the healing process is to forgive the person that harmed me, no matter what the damage.

So, that's what I was determined to do.

I had one more person to forgive. I knew that it was going to take some time. There was still a lot of friction going on between me and Mom. I was never happy with her. I always felt life was about her. I didn't feel I was an important part of her life. But this whole cancer thing was changing that. I was willing to do the work to get through the emotional garbage. I knew she was too. If that was one of the gifts cancer gave me, then I'd be grateful. I had a fleeting thought: *I could go to my grave knowing that I have peace in my heart.* When all is forgiven, peace has a place to enter.

This thought process was quickly erased from my mind. What you think and what you believe go a long way to the outcome you want. I wasn't done with this fight, not by a long shot. But I had just experienced a major victory. I had challenges, disappointments, and I'd allowed others to control me—my ex, my mother, my grandmother. But the real victory was I finally had forgiveness, blessings, and health *today*.

Positivity (With Intention And A Great Big Helping Of Humor)

CHAPTER 7

The First Good News

I was apprehensive as hell about going back to the doctor. I'd spent at least two weeks before the appointment visualizing what I wanted the outcome to be. I kept seeing myself well, but I began to allow doubt to enter my mind. *Do these alternative practitioners really know what they're talking about? Should I have done chemo? And why is my spleen larger? Why is there a new rash?* The questions came fast and furious. "Laurie, just shut up," I told myself. That worked for a while—all of five minutes. I was trying everyone's nerves. Boston loomed in my mind.

And then I board the plane.

I was scheduled for a CT scan—another one of those scary tests that I never wanted to experience. The procedure is to drink three bottles of Crystal Light with some kind of glowing medicine in it. Great. As a rule, I don't drink anything with aspartame in it. It could cause cancer. *Oops, I already have that, so what's the big deal?* I tried to find out if the Crystal Light would make me feel weird. My darling sons reminded me I was already weird, so I decided to just go through with the test. God knows I'd been through hell and back already. It couldn't taste anything as bad as the herbs I consumed daily.

When we got to the doctor's, I drank my Crystal Light like a good girl. As I drank it, my mom just stared at me. At the time, I figured she was thinking, *How could that possibly be good for her if it makes part of her body glow under a machine.* The attendants took me to the machine that would encapsulate me. At that point, I was still more than a little claustrophobic, and that idea scared me even more. What I wanted to do was run, run away to another country and make this whole thing disappear. I didn't think they would let me at that point, so I got on the stretcher, and into the machine I went.

When they put me into the machine, my body was shaking. I was scared to death until I looked up and saw hand-painted clouds on the ceiling. A huge sense of calm came over me. The clouds paralleled the outside world, a place that represented health. I was immediately taken to the space I so coveted, my chi walks. I decided I would walk in those clouds, enjoy God's creation of the sky and stars, and feel the breeze on my face washing away all the sickness.

The technician handling my scan was very sweet. She explained that they would inject a dye throughout my body. I wanted to protest, but thought better of it. They needed this test to find out what was going on deep in my body. I had an IV in my arm, and the technician told me that as the dye went into my veins, I would feel a warm sensation, almost like I had to pee. It would all be over in three minutes. *Damn, I can do anything for three minutes!*

Finally, the test started They slid me back and forth two times through an open donut dome—and poof, I was done. Another test conquered. The text results were practically instantaneous. Thank God I didn't have to wait days to hear. In about an hour, I was called back into an examination room. I took a deep breath, visualized what I wanted one more time, and said to Mom, "It's show time."

The doctors entered the room shortly after we sat down. The first fellow did a quick exam and then the big man, Dr. Fisher, took his turn. They smiled and asked me the usual questions, and then Dr. Fisher said, "Let's read your results."

I took another deep breath. So did Mom. "Let's do the good news first. Your blood count, which was off the charts at 70,000 plus. It's...now...11,000." He slowed way down on the last number. There was a different tone in his voice—half way between unbelief and awe. (The normal white blood cell count is between 4,000 and 11,000.) I later had Tyler, who was in a pre-med program, give my initial blood work to his professor. I wanted to know what the deal was from that perspective. His professor looked at the results, then looked at Ty, and asked, "Is this person still alive?"

I was thinking, *Yes, it's gone! Can I go home now?*

Not quite. They read my baseline CT scan. Lymph nodes are 60 percent swollen throughout my body, and my spleen was extremely enlarged. I didn't need to drink glow-in-the-dark Kool-Aid to find that out; it was bulging out of my stomach.

We talked for a bit more. They told me the same thing they had last time: "We'll see you in three months." No chemo again! Dr. Fisher based his reasoning, again, on the fact that I wasn't having night sweats. I had not lost my appetite, although I had dropped some weight—some of that was needed and definitely not enough to be concerned about. And I was still getting out of bed and going about my day.

I was thrilled. It was like I was getting another "get out of jail" card. I was used to this watchful waiting bit—it was familiar, and I could do it. Mom and I looked at each other, still unable to fully believe what we were hearing. I didn't understand how amazing it was that my blood cell count was back in a normal range. What I kept hearing was what Dr. Fisher said: "We're saving your magic bullets. ...Three more months of watchful waiting." I also wondered what the magic bullets were—the chemo or all the "work" I'd done up to that moment. But it didn't matter.

Mom and I celebrated my progress. It was the first glimmer of hope I'd had since the whole ordeal began. I was obviously doing something right, but I wasn't out of the soup yet. I left Boston ready to hunker down. The real work was about to begin.

Laurie's Research Center for Healing

Once I got home, I decided to get down to business. I knew that I should keep doing exactly what I had been doing all along. More tea—including the gas that went with it—more walks, more needles, more energy work. I was very skeptical about what my Western medical doctors were telling me about food. Dr. Fisher mentioned that more and more women were getting this type of cancer, and they didn't see any correlation between diet and lymphoma. The first part made me sit up and take notice, and the second part didn't feel right. I didn't think—and still don't— they were looking closely enough. I do believe that keeping your immune system strong is very important. This comes with a balanced diet, exercise, and positive messages in one's mind. To me, this means mind, body, and spirit. You can't have one without the others.

I wanted to know more about how that connection works. When I first got my diagnosis, my mother sent me a stack of books. She knew a lot of experts in the mind-body-spirit field, and she herself is a recognized expert on the effects of stress on the body. I read her books and those she recommended to me. Yet I hungered for more. I started ordering books by the truckload—UPS seemed to show up at my house daily. Soon my UPS driver knew all about what I was doing. I became a mad scientist surfing the Internet and looking at all the different healing modalities out there. I knew that most important was keeping a healthy mindset, but I needed to understand. Why did I get this type of cancer? What had I been exposed to?

I started the organic extravaganza. Bob never knew what concoction was going to show up on his plate, and it became a fun game for us. But the more I learned about most of the food we eat, the more I wondered why everyone on the planet — or at least in the United States — isn't sick.

If you don't eat organic, you're polluting your body regularly with all the toxins in and on our food. Fruits and veggies are supposed to be good for you, but how could they be when they're sprayed with nasty chemical pesticides to kill bugs and with herbicides to kill weeds. Seeds have been genetically modified to make the produce less attractive to bugs, but what does that do to the actual food that we're eating? Does our body reject it in some way? Yes, I found out. To keep the produce fresh longer, they irradiate it — that means that they put radiation in our food. While this is supposed to be "safe," I wonder how anyone could say that when the long-term effect of exposure to low doses of radiation in the body isn't known.

The meat we consume is a crapshoot, being factory-raised meat. The feed is loaded with the same pesticides and herbicides we're consuming on our produce, and who knows what kind of chemical change happens when the chemically laden corn and whatever else the livestock eat is converted into muscle and fat. I believe those chemicals get lodged in the fat that we then consume. To make matters worse, it's loaded with hormones to make the cows, chickens, pigs, and sheep bigger. It's believed that hormones in meat are making our children mature far younger than ever before; some girls are getting their menses at the age of eight. Never mind that the hormones in meat can make tumors grow more rapidly; that is a known fact.

I'm sure you've heard that the amount of rat feces in some food is regulated — like it should be there at all. But what happens when chickens are processed grosses me out. I remember at Grannie's farm, she'd pick out a chicken and have them kill it right in front of her. But major chicken producers first load the chickens with antibiotics to keep respiratory infections down — and, yes, that's passed to us through the meat. Though they vacuum out the phlegm in the lungs before processing, they don't do much about all the excrement that covers the skin. When any animal is kept in close confinement with other animals, they defecate on each other. Where else are they supposed to go? They used to take the skin off. Then they decided that washing it with soap and water was fine. Now, apparently, that's too expensive, so they just rinse the parasite and bacterial-laden chicken with water. No wonder there are more incidences of E. coli.

I also found out that it's not just the bad stuff we're putting into our bodies but the stuff we put *on* our bodies that can harm us—even the very air we breathe can be full of chemicals. Ever read what's in laundry soap? The perfumes and dyes can be very harmful, because many people don't realize the huge role our skin plays. Next to the liver, it's the largest detox organ in the body. Our skin eliminates toxins in the form of sweat. But skin is cellular, meaning things can soak into it as well as sweat out of it. Perfumes, dyes, pesticides, and herbicides we use on our lawns to keep them free from dandelions and spiders, and even the everyday cleaning chemicals we use permeate our skin and get into our cells. I also found out that there are harmful chemicals in rugs, paint, new furniture, and much more.

Even our water can harm us if it's not filtered. The chlorine used to kill germs is necessary, because we need a clean water supply. But it's important to filter it out before you drink it or shower with it. Add to these all our unhealthy lifestyles—smoking, drinking too much, overeating—it's a recipe for disaster. I'm glad I found out early, not just about the problems but how to fix them.

Today there are eco-friendly options, such as companies like Seventh Generation and Eco, which make laundry detergent that gets your clothes just as clean as major brands (especially if you throw in a little bit of perfume- and dye-free OxiClean). Cleaning a house with plant-based cleaners has gotten easier in the past few years. Visit any health food store, and you'll see an entire grocery aisle dedicated to cleaning products. If you don't have a health-food store in town, good old vinegar and water does a bang-em-up job cleaning hard surface, floors, and toilets. (Here's a fun tip: Heat a large pan of water on the stove with about one-third vinegar and two-thirds water. When it's steaming, pour it into the toilet—not enough to make the toilet flush, but just enough to fill it. Let it sit for a few minutes, and then swipe it out with a toilet brush. It's as clean as Mr. Bubble could ever make it—and just as germ free, because you're using hot water! How cool is that?)

The real push behind all of the research into foods and such was that I needed to figure out what benefits and what harms the lymphatic system. Specifically, what foods like cancer? What was polluting my body? I came up with a do and don't list. The do's for me include changing my diet to primarily vegetarian—mostly veggies, fruits, and grains—and if I do eat meat, it has to be organic. Hormone-infused meat is out of the question, as is dairy. Dairy is very difficult for most adults to digest, and while cheese is a beautiful food, its health benefits are minimal. I basically eat like we did about a hundred years ago, and I have one motto with food: "Keep it simple." I don't eat processed foods, which generally is any kind of food that has been changed into its current form and that comes in a package in the grocery store. Junk food is an obvious example, but even things like cereal and string cheese are considered processed by hard-core folks. I also follow a yeast-free diet as much as possible: no sugar, nothing fermented or cultured. If cancer is caused by an underlying infection, and since systemic yeast, mold, and fungus infections are common underlying infections in most people, why chance it? It is hard not to eat bread and even cheese. But I'll admit I've had an occasional glass of wine.

After a couple of trips to the grocery store with my new shopping list in hand, I had to laugh. I had gone back to Grannie's way of eating. I resented the hell out of it as a child, but there I was, buying everything fresh and cooking from scratch. I only shopped the perimeter of the market—the packaged stuff was found in the interior part of the aisle. I also consciously switched all of my cleaning products to those that are plant based—if it had the word *surfactant* in its list, I didn't buy it. And the only acceptable fragrance was from essential oils. I even stopped using anything but organic fertilizer on my lawn. I found some great recipes on the Net for killing weeds. My favorite is made with beer and Dawn dishwashing soap.

I read the labels on everything. I won't buy it if it has any chemicals or preservatives in it. In other words, I've become a food czar. Sound extreme? You bet. I try not to be ridiculous about it. If we go out to a restaurant, I eat fish. (Buffalo is also a good choice. They can't factory farm buffalo—these magnificent animals live and eat like they have done for thousands of years. It's a very safe and healthy meat.) Is it hard? Yes, but it's my life I'm fighting for, and to this day if it calls for some extreme measures, so be it.

I wanted to find out if there were more things I could do, so I searched and searched.

I spent hours on the Internet researching what was out there. There was a machine invented by a Mr. Rife that's a supposed to be secret. Somehow, it's supposed work with high-frequency something or other, and it looked like it would move energy through the body. It sounded intriguing, but so did a lot of other things. I decided that investing thousands of dollars on a not-for-sure outcome wasn't the way to go. I used infrared lights, which can penetrate to the cellular level. I tried infrared saunas and found out there's also Mecon beds, lasers, and all sorts of things that affect the cells. I even found a detoxifying foot bath that's supposed to pull toxins out of the body. I figured I was detoxing like nobody's business with the herbs, so any additional detoxing couldn't hurt. I even read about colonics, where you drink stuff that sounds like a cocktail drink to me. While colonics can give any detox program a huge boost—it's good to rid the bowels of old putrid matter—I didn't do the cocktails or the colonics, though I do know people who have and who rave about them.

I discovered the harmful effects of EMFs (electromagnetic fields). These are simply the physical field produced by electrically charged objects. They can be harmful in high doses. They affect your pineal gland, a small gland in the middle of your head that produces melatonin. When your pineal gland is weakened, your immune system is affected, so EMFs can be very harmful. I also learned they're everywhere — from computers and cell phones to appliances and even in some electrical outlets. If you live close to an electrical switching station — points on the electric grid where the energy passes through — or if your bedroom is too close to the electrical input into the house, you could be bombarded by high amounts of EMFs. Even an LED alarm clock is potentially dangerous. I learned that you should keep an LED alarm clock at least three feet away from your head.

I tried whatever sounded right to me. That's about as scientific as alchemy (the old "magic" of turning everyday stuff like straw into gold), but it was a very good guide for me. I put a crystal on my computer to soak up the EMF rays. I also tried to get at least twenty minutes of sunshine in my eyes — without sunglasses, glasses, even contacts — to strengthen my pineal gland and get vital vitamin D.

Oh, and I read. And read. And read some more. I read Lance Armstrong's book *It's Not About the Bike* the first night I got my news. That alone inspired me to conquer whatever they were telling me — well, sort of. If he could survive testicular cancer that spread to his brain, then I thought, *I've got a chance.* At that early stage of the game, I needed to know that. I also recognized that he had a strong team of advocates around him, and it made me feel strong just knowing I had my team.

Another very helpful book I read early on was *Healing at the Cellular Level* by Vicky Thompson. It explains how we can create disease in our bodies with just our thoughts. Because I read it before I met with Alice, I knew that what she was saying had validity. The author also showed how cells shift and change in our body every four months and how stress can make cells go crazy. Good cells fight off bad ones, and this was vital information for me during my healing work. I also liked the scientific approach to what she was saying, and I read the book more than a couple of times. I read Christian books, Buddhist books — you name it. If it had to do with cancer and/or healing, I read it. Louise Hayes's book *You Can Heal Your Body* became my Bible. I had read it over fifteen years before, but her message hadn't registered then — or maybe I just didn't need it at the time.

Hayes's work is based on the integrative approach. She first talks about integrating the mind and the body. She says — and I believe her — that our organs are very sensitive to our emotions. Each emotion plays a big part in how our body reacts to things. From stuffing feelings to resentment to anger or fear, each of these emotions can create pain in the body, from superficial pain to disease pertaining to each organ. It was, like *Cellular Level*, prepping me for all the alternative work I was about to embark on.

* Every thought we think is creating our future.
* The point of power is always in the present moment.
* Everyone suffers from self-hatred and guilt.
* It is only a thought and a thought can be changed.
* We help create so called illness in our bodies.
* Resentment, criticism, and guilt are the most damaging patterns [God help me, I had all three in spades!]
* Releasing resentment will dissolve cancer. [This still gives me chill bumps.] I let go of all resentment whatever or whomever it was attached to.
* We must release and forgive everyone. You can forgive but never forget.
* We must be willing to begin to love ourselves.
* Self-approval and self-acceptance in the now are the keys to positive changes.
* When we love ourselves, everything in our life works better.

Integrating Western and Alternative Modes of Healing

But what's still important, is that I was able to take Hayes's idea of integration and transfer the knowledge. I felt very strongly about integrating Western medicine with alternative, mostly Eastern-based healing modalities. I felt there was a reason and a legitimate purpose for both purposes. I was lucky I was able to handle my cancer with alternative methods. However, I was well aware that if certain things started happening—if I started getting way too short of breath just by taking a short walk or if all of a sudden I just couldn't get out of bed—then it was time to get another test. I also resolved that if Dr. Fisher recommended that I needed chemo, I would do it. It was even more important to know that all the alternative things I was doing would support me through chemo.

Western medicine has come a long way. I always say, if my arm is severed in an accident, I'm going to the hospital to get it sewn back on. Chinese medicine wouldn't be able to sew it back on. I would never tell anyone with my diagnosis to use *only* alternative healing methods. I know how important it is to gather as much information as possible in the time frame you have to make the best decision. Above all, it is vital to be tested and to use chemo or radiation if necessary. Cancer is a highly unpredictable disease, and you want to throw at it every weapon available in your arsenal when needed.

My Support System

After I returned from Boston the second time, I made the next three months all about me—again. I sat my family down and said, "I love you all, but I also love myself." This was a true revelation; just saying it was powerful. I told my sons and my husband that I wanted to live and be around for a long time. "So here's what I need from you," I bravely told them.

I struggled with that concept for so long. In my delusional mind, asking for what I needed meant they didn't already know what I needed, which made me feel resentful. How unbelievably silly—no one can read minds. So, I gave them my lists of needs and wants: no negative messages, no tension, no fighting, stay out of trouble (that one was for Nick and Ty), send me lots of love, pray lots of prayers, be the best you can be, and let me do what I need to do. I told them sternly. "If you want to make only negative or snide comments, say them to each other, but keep them to yourself. I'm on a mission." They all gave me a salute and a "yes, sir." I knew that I had reached them at their core.

Bless their dear hearts, they did help me. Bob was his usual supportive self, and he was very honest with me — something that was also very important. He told me when he was scared — sometimes petrified. Our anniversary fell in the second three-month, watchful waiting period, and it still amazes me when I read what he wrote to me on that day:

> Selfishly I'm afraid of you leaving me and ending up broken hearted and alone. There is no way you can really understand how real and frightening that is for me. You know I'm fearless, but this terrifies me. You see I need you in so many ways. You are my friend, my grounding, my partner, and my angel. You are God's earth angel too, I know that for sure. If you imagined what an angel on earth would look like...look in the mirror. People, animals, and just about anything else that is alive is attracted to you. Not because of your looks, but for who you are and your heart. You make me better in every way. You make me more handsome, more successful, a better person, and you motivate me to do so much. My life is not worth living without you. My only fear is God might want his earth angel and he might need you more than I do. I know he has a plan on earth and heaven for you. My prayers are for the next twelve years and the next twelve years after that! I love you, Laurie Beck.

Because of Bob's honesty, we were able to talk about things I might have otherwise kept stuffed within me. At our anniversary dinner, I told him that I was a little resentful. I had trained him into being a decent husband, and if the cancer did take me, another woman would get to enjoy the rewards of all my hard work. It sounded odd, but it was something that I needed to say. And once it was out in the open, it was so much easier to deal with. We still laugh about it today.

My entire family was amazing through the whole process. They rallied around me. My dad, whom I feel wasn't nurturing enough when I was a girl, gave me the love and attention I had craved as a child. My brothers made sure I knew how much they loved me. And above all, my mom had my best interest at heart. Cancer is devastating, but it is the catalyst that healed my relationship with Mom. We let go of the past and began a true friendship.

Alice and I spent hours and hours going through so much stuff about my mother. I had to go really deep to get past the abandonment issue and all the anger and resentment. It was so freeing to realize what was going on. Mom was always trying to escape an unhappy place, which in turn created the same feelings for me, and that was the key. It didn't matter what haunted my mother. It only mattered how it affected me. I had to disassociate what was going on with my mother and the effect it created in me. Once I had that distance, the floodgates open. I recognized that I was always running from something, that I didn't know how something was supposed to feel, even if it was good.

I didn't know how to sort out my emotions. They seemed so scrambled. If something felt good, I questioned it. If somebody did something nice, I thought there was some hidden meaning behind it. I felt that everyone—mostly my grandmother and mother and Jake—always attached a price to any good deed, whether it was emotional or financial. I resented that my mother was emotionally unavailable to me as a child and physically unavailable when I was older. When I was young and staying at Grannie's, I begged her to come. She would always have an excuse why she couldn't. When I became a mother, my mother was noticeably absent. I resented that absence until I learned to let it go. Mom was trying to survive like the rest of us. She had her own demons to confront.

But all of that doesn't matter anymore. With Alice's help, I let it all go—the anger, the resentment, the guilt. I was resentful when my mother told me to get acupuncture when I first called to tell her the news. I think what really happened was that something shifted in her universe. She was wonderful and supportive.

She embarked on a huge fact-finding mission to help me heal. She talked to everyone she knew — and she knew a lot of people. She read as many books as I did. She became my advocate, my watchdog. She became a real mom. And this continues to be the case up to this very day.

We did have a rough time together throughout most of our lives. She is still my mother, so we do have our disagreements. But that doesn't matter, because we've made our peace and are able to move forward together. Once my mother and I made our peace, and I was able to forgive all the perceived wrongs, things started moving in the right direction.

The Daily Routine

I also had a routine that I followed without fail. It incorporated everything I had learned up to that point — my second period of watchful waiting.

I knew I had two choices when I started my day. It was either going to be a great day or it was going to be a struggle. Ninety percent of the time, I chose to seize the day. It didn't matter that I had constant visual reminders that all was not well with my body: my spleen continued to bulge out of my belly; I have big lumps on the back of my neck. I had a hard time breathing, and my ear was constantly clogged. Rather than being fearful of what was wrong, I chose to honor each one. I thanked my spleen, my ear, those lumps on my neck — whatever was manifesting disease — for making me aware that I needed to change certain practices in my life. I looked at or felt each area, said " hello," and let my body know I was working hard to heal those areas. Most importantly, I was working hard at healing my life. I knew I had a lot of sadness, anger, and resentment, but I was no different from a lot of other people with the same issues. I took the responsibility for turning my baggage into cancer.

Taking responsibility for my life and how I chose to live took a huge weight off my shoulders. I spent so much time trying to blame others. It wasn't my mom's fault or my Granny's fault, my ex-husband's fault, or anyone else's fault that I was in this predicament. It was my " realization of responsibility," and if I got myself into it, I'd better damn well make sure I was working to get myself out of it.

The minute I opened my eyes, I thanked God for the day. I still say that at least fifty times or so every day. I thanked him for my health, my life, my children, my husband, my friends, my dogs — anyone and everyone who was important to me. Then I'd go down and make my morning coffee. Don't tell Summer this — my herbalist, the woman partly responsible for all these concoctions I am drinking. She'll be horrified if she finds out. Coffee is definitely a big no-no in Chinese medicine. I was drinking my thirty ounces of nasty herbs every day, and I wasn't giving up my one cup a day or my one glass of wine in the evening. I enjoyed both, and that enjoyment was very important during that time. (The coffee was organic and fresh ground — no extra chemicals and tasted great.)

After my coffee, I went back to bed and spent thirty minutes scanning my body. I'd go in my mind to all the areas that I knew were affected. I had asked my doctors for the hard copies of my tests so I could read my results, which was both a good and a bad idea. I needed to know what was going on in my body. I knew my spleen was extremely enlarged. If it didn't get better by the next visit, they would recommend chemo. But I was going to do everything in my power to avoid chemo. In my morning scan, I searched for any part that was swollen. I'd spend a good ten minutes on my spleen. I'd tell it, "Okay, spleen, so let's get busy." I'd send my spleen smiley faces, red hearts, and lots of *love*. Right after I got back from my second visit to Boston, I had an aha moment with my acupuncturist. I asked her if there was anything we could do to make my spleen shrink.

She replied, "That's simple. Just send it *love*."

I thought about that for a moment, and she must have seen a confused look on my face, because she added, "When we obsess about something, we make it bigger. When we send it love, it shrinks." Brilliant. I had an infinite amount of love to give my body. I had never really loved it before, but only punished it for being fat or slow or whatever. I was determined to send it as much love as it needed.

After I spent some time on my spleen, I visualized all sorts of wacky but very helpful things. Up until that point, I'd only known about visualization from sports; successful athletes use visualization all the time. I grew up training horses, so I was an athlete. I jumped five-foot fences and thought nothing of it, but no matter how hard I tried to see myself jumping through the horse course, I couldn't do it. My wonderful Alice taught me some fabulous techniques that I use every day still when I need them.

First I visualized my body healing any and every cell. That was pretty standard. But depending on the day, sometimes I visualized putting a suit of armor on the good cells and having them battle with the bad cells. Or I imagine bulldozers in my body, building a foundation and plowing down the old, taking away all the damaged debris. Sometimes I visualized walls to keep the good cells in and the bad cells out.

Part of my research was in cellular regeneration. I wanted to know how cells reproduce themselves over and over, so I could help them regenerate in a healthy way. I wished I had paid better attention in biology class. I constantly visualized new and healthy growth for my cells. Many times I had the Archangel Michael, Prince of Light, who fights against evil, come in with his swords and cut and slice away any bad cells or growing tumors. I used any images I could conjure up to get that cancer out of my body and replace it with healthy cells.

Once I finish my visualization of fighting the cancer, I visualized a violet light. Alice taught me that to some violet light is a healing light. I came to know it as a pure crystal liquid that I infused throughout my body, sending it wherever it needed to go—my lymph system, the lumps in my neck, the rashes on my body, and of course my spleen. I thought of the violet light as the cancer's kryptonite. As I infused my spleen with violet light, I placed my hands over it and felt the warmth of my hands giving love to my body. It was exciting; I was so used to sending negative messages that I got tingly when I did it. I then sent more love to my spleen. I visualized hearts and happy faces all around it—whatever it took to let it know I loved it and that it was important to my body and spirit.

Then I visualized finding happy or peaceful places. Sometimes I saw myself lying on the beach. The water from the ocean was navigating up into my body to the crown of my head and then rinsing out all toxins. I mentally washed each organ one at a time and sent each one love. I visualized my horse, Jake, taking me on special rides to memorable places. We had a very special bond, and he had passed on a few years prior to my illness. I used him a lot in my visualizations at Alice's office. She wanted me to find happy places in the midst of all the muck we were working through.

I took what happened in April's office and made it part of my daily routine. Jake and I would go to open fields with daises all around us. Sometimes we just charged down the beach, feeling free and alive. Even though his body had been buried long before in the front yard of our Atlanta home, I still felt him in spirit. His power and strength had been a major part of my life for twenty-three years—some of the worst years of my life. We loved each other through thick and thin when he was alive. I knew he was taking care of me still.

After I finished, sometimes I felt totally energized, and sometimes I felt Zen-like—peaceful and accepting of everything. As I did my "body work" as Bob started to call it, I got different sensations in my body. Many times, I didn't know if they were good or bad, but that didn't stop me. I just kept doing my work every morning—and even during the day if I start getting upset. I don't know how many times Bob said to me, "Go lie down and do your stuff," if I was having a hard time.

It was amazing, actually, how much he supported my time and space to do that body work. If Bob doesn't know how something works, he often becomes relentless, and it gets worse if there's no empirical explanation for what's going on. But my honey never ceased to amaze me; the one time I really needed him to allow me to be and not to criticize or make nasty or deriding comments, he stepped up to the plate and came through. He knew that he needed to respect that I didn't know how much longer I had. If I had X amount of time, I wanted to live it the way I wanted to live it—not his way. I am forever grateful to him for that, and now that we're on the other side, I find that it has carried forward into the future. He is much more understanding and encouraging about any harebrained scheme I cook up. If I'm counting the gifts that appear with adversity, this is definitely one of them.

After I finished my visualization work, I spent the rest of the day making my tea, taking chi walks, and thinking positive thoughts all the time. I made a healthy lunch, took a nap, read, did some more healing work, made dinner, read, and went to bed doing some breath work—visualizing the bad cells exhaling out of my body, of course. Once a week, I got acupuncture and Reiki, and visited Alice for more energy work. It sounds pretty simple, but I had terrorizing thoughts bombarding me. It took a lot of intention and a lot of concentration to keep up my daily routine day after day.

I knew I wasn't alone, even in the darkest time. I gave my illness requests to God. I knew that He has a plan for me. I needed to learn to let go and trust the process—just like when I get on a plane, I have to turn over the outcome to someone else. When I accepted that I wasn't in charge of flying that plane, no matter how much I thought I could control the outcome, it was so freeing to let go. Above all, I needed to trust that what I was doing was working. My blood count going back into normal range was the first encouraging sign.

Soon after I returned from Boson the second time, I also decide it was time to get back into my studio and start giving back again. I decided early on to do only forms of exercise that made me feel good, like Pilates and walking. I always focused on my breathing in conjunction with positive thoughts, but I had become a bit reclusive, so I needed to let people know I was okay. I loved my clients and I loved to teach.

The day I stepped back into the studio, it was like I'd forgotten how to teach. I had to think about each question, each Pilates pose. It was like I have amnesia. On the first day, I did three hours then went home and took a nap. But I felt invigorated, and so I did it a little more the next day. I was reconnecting and starting to share, and that was powerful. Everyone was wondering what I was doing, because when cancer is in your blood, lymph, and internal organs like your spleen, it's never good. I'm sure they were thinking, *Let's support Laurie while she's still here.* Now I laugh. Whether this was true or not, I felt like I got to teach "sympathy Pilates" for a while. I thought, *I've gone from being the best in town to being the cause de jour.* People never said this; these are my crazy thoughts. But it played in the back of my mind that my neighbor doctor thought I should be dead, and I'm sure he told people as much. I do know that I made my clients think about their own lives, their own mortality. And they were all very supportive. I've kept all the cards they sent to me to give me encouragement and support.

Paying Attention

As I settled into my routine, I started to believe that the mind is far more powerful than I had ever given it credit for. I decided to do a little test on myself. Test number one: when I would feel a twinge in my body, especially around my spleen area, I would either terrorize myself or acknowledge that it was reminding to me to slow down. When I terrorized myself, it ached more — sometimes painfully. When I acknowledged that it was telling me to slow down, it would stop. Sometimes days would go by with a constant sensation there. Interesting. I decide to up the ante. When it ached, I paid attention to my thoughts. Generally they were

- Am I getting sicker?
- What did I do to aggravate it today?
- Did I overdo it?
- Am I allowing my husband and/or sons to stress me?
- Is it spreading?
- Is it getting larger?

Once I knew what I was thinking, I decided to change my thoughts to

- Laurie, you need to slow down.
- Whatever just occurred is not a big deal.
- My body is telling me something.
- My spleen is affected by my emotions.
- I love my spleen.
- My spleen is healthy and whole.
- My body is a temple.
- I love my body.

The minute I changed my thoughts, I felt the sensations subside. Funny how that works.

I also started to pay very close attention to stress. When I get stressed out, I am harming my body. Stress takes such a horrible toll on the body. If I felt stress coming on, I immediately felt that twinge in my spleen. I would also get intense headaches or migraines. When I started paying attention to what was causing me stress, I realized that I could internalize things so hard core or blow them so far out of proportion that I literally created shortness of breath. Then I started paying attention to what happened when I felt fear. I looked at the issue of flying. It used to be that the minute they closed the door, I would feel my armpits starting to sweat profusely. How apropos that I discovered the lumps in my armpits, and this condition is in my lymphatic system.

It was all starting to make perfect sense. And the good news is, I'm not afraid to fly anymore. My positive intentions, with a help from the Big Guy in heaven, took care of that. I simply decided there are more important things to think about. Most important is something I discovered in all my mind-body-spirit work: I needed to give it up. I was not in total control of this situation. I said the Serenity Prayer several times a day. What I did discover is that there are some things I do control. I can choose to say that prayer, think only positive thoughts, take care of my body, drink my herbs, and do my chi walking, my energy work, my Pilates. The list was long, but I felt empowered. I learned I can follow my heart and not listen to chatter. I can KISS: keep it simple, stupid. I have my program. I followed it religiously, no matter what I was thinking or fearing or worried about. I had the support of my wonderful husband, my sons, my brothers, father, mother, and friends. I still had questions, fears, doubts, as I move closer to my next appointment. I knew something was going right.

Fifth Time's a Charm

The next visit was approaching. I started practicing weeks ahead, visualizing how I wanted it to go. I navigated through my tests; heard the doctors telling me good news; and then saw me departing for home not heaven. When I get to Boston, I did my tests. My white blood cell count had dropped drastically, but they still weren't back to normal. My lymphatic system was still compromised. That one was no big surprise. I knew I still had tumors in my lung region, abdomen, and groin area, and my spleen was still extremely enlarged — but not enlarged enough to do chemo. So I got my "get out of jail" card again. Three more months of watching, worrying, being positive, and living. It wasn't the news I wanted, but it wasn't the news I dreaded.

I went back home from Boston after the third visit resolved to work even harder. I did more body work than I had before. My intentions grew stronger by the day. I decided that I was in it... for my life!

I worked hard this time focusing all energies on my spleen and lymph nodes. I threw at it all the ammunition I could find. Again I know the most important tool was my mind. There were times I went to the darkest, deepest, worst places in my mind. I experienced fear so overwhelming it paralyzed my breath. Literally, I became short of breath and then couldn't take a breath. My thoughts race. *I don't want to die. I am finally living!*

I had all these bottled-up emotions. The more work I did with Alice, the more peaceful I felt. The only apprehension I felt was when I thought about going back to the cancer hospital for more tests. But I didn't concentrate on the next visit. Instead, I focused on all the good that was happening. I was starting to feel free and that I could do anything. I definitely reaffirmed that I wanted to be here longer, to see what I had to offer this beautiful planet. I wanted to make a difference. I wanted to continue to touch lives, to love openly and passionately. I wanted to make an apple pie in the fall for as many falls as possible. I wanted to ride horses and just to keep living. *Thank you, God, for the gift of life,* I repeated daily.

I sent as much love to my spleen and lymph system as I could muster. My spleen needed its swelling to subside — or even return to its normal state. If not, the doctor said he'd have to operate. I also didn't want to start the chemo route, knowing I only had a small chance of success.

Finally, it was time to go back for my fourth visit. I waited six weeks before going — I don't know why. Maybe I just want to be damn sure that I was going to get a different report this time.

The fourth visit was feeling a bit uncertain to me, at least more than the last one. I started doubting my decision to wait another month and a half to go. I even started getting afraid. *Maybe I should have listened and returned in three months.* I rehashed the reasons I didn't go back in three months. *Life sometimes gets in the way of any schedule,* I told myself. Flying to Boston regularly wasn't easy from where I lived. It took a whole day to fly to Boston from Florida and then another day to travel to Dana Farber to see the doctors. I could create many excuses when needed, and I had a lot of reasons why I didn't need to get on a plane. Oddly, I didn't know why I was so apprehensive about flying again. Mom and I had our routine down. I intellectually know that the plane wasn't going to blow up when the door closed. I finally had to confront the inevitable. I was fearful of what the tests may reveal.

As my appointment drew near, my mind was racing like a horse in the starting gate. When I meet Mom at the airport, my palms were sweating, and I was extremely quiet. The next day, we woke up early as usual and went on our way to the hospital, but our ride into Boston seemed longer than usual. Mom kept trying to make small talk, but my answers were short and concise. I was in preparation mode; my thoughts raced; my body shook. I felt like I was in solitary confinement — dark and closed in — not good if you're a claustrophobic freak. I felt hypersensitive to sounds as well. I felt like the volume was turned up on my mom's voice, and I was in a deep well.

We finally made it to the hospital. And I knew the drill all too well. The worst part was the waiting. I waited in the waiting room, I waited in the hematology room, I waited in the vital statistics room, I waited in the doctor's room. I hate waiting! I just wanted to know *now*.

When Mom and I finally made it into the doctor's room, we waited the longest we ever had to wait. Mom began to lose her patience. She wasn't a quiet, sit-and-wait kinda Mom. She would have the whole hospital jumping and fetching if she felt the need. I kept telling her, "Mom, relax." Ha, easy for me to say. Finally, an hour later, Dr. Fisher walked in. *Oh no, he has someone else with him. Oh God, what does this mean?*

Dr. Fisher greeted us with his usual calm presence. He introduced the man, a doctor from Spain. My mind immediately started jumping to conclusions. *Why is there a foreign doctor in my room? Do I now have some sort of foreign lymphoma? Was it that extra month that I waited?*

I said, "That's nice. Can I have my results please?"

Dr. Fisher smiled and said, "Laurie, everything looks great. Your blood is perfect, just like a person that's healthy." This floored me, and immediately I felt some of the enormous weight I'd carried around with me for ten months lift, just a little. Because of that good news, I got bold. I looked at him and said, "I think I have more amazing news. Will you check my spleen?"

He checked my spleen and said yes, it had gone down. I let out a mental whoopee. I don't know why I restrained myself. Finally, I had some news that I could celebrate.

We talked a bit more, and he said, "This time I'm extending your visit to six months. Your body is healing, and it is amazing." It's hard to read Dr. Fisher. I bet he's one hell of a poker player. But I think I detected something in his look—amazement, pride, relief. Who knows?

Mom and I did our usual look at each other. I knew she was even more relieved than I was. I knew these visits were equally if not more torturous for her than for me. Can you imagine being in one of the sickest hospitals in the country with your only daughter, who has, by all definitions, terminal cancer? I hope I never have to even imagine such darkness.

I will always cherish the smile my mom gave me at that moment. It radiated pure love, pure acknowledgement. It's the best smile she has ever given me.

I went home, more determined than ever. It was the same routine — brewing, walking, acupuncture, Alice, and constant affirmations and visualizations. But this time I knew it was working. That made all my mental work a thousand times more powerful.

I worked ten times harder as the next six months passed — the same grueling journey. This time my spleen had gone down even more. I could feel the difference. This made me feel *really* confident. I also felt the lumps in my neck and my groin going down. This added TNT to all the healing work I was doing. I was starting to feel powerful, something I'd never fully felt before.

After I had all the tests again and waited the requisite multiple hours for everyone, Dr. Fisher finally walked into the examination room. This time he was alone. He immediately said, "Laurie, everything is clean. Your blood is the cleanest I've ever seen it."

At that moment, I just looked at him. I couldn't believe it. I didn't know if my mom could either. Because I want to make sure I was hearing it all correctly. I ask Dr. Fisher what that meant. He said, again, "Your blood is clean. Your lymph is clean. That means that you don't have to come back for a year if you don't want to. Keep doing whatever you've been doing though. Don't stop that now."

I was uncomfortable waiting a full year before seeing Dr. Fisher again, and I told him. I knew I'd start stressing out about everything — after all, not knowing can kill a person. Our cells change every three months, and I didn't want a relapse from the progress that I'd made. Dr. Fisher said a six-month checkup would be fine.

The next six months were a breeze compared to what I had been through the past year and a half. I kept up with all my healing therapies and had every intention of staying well. So I started visualizing what the good doctor was going to say at the next checkup.

In May of 2009, I scheduled that six-month checkup. Same grueling flight. Same excruciating wait. Dr. Fisher walked into the exam room. "Laurie, we can't find any cancer anywhere," he announced to my mother and me.

I didn't want to read anything into what he was saying, so as I had done many times before, I asked him what this meant.

"We can't find it. It's not showing up anywhere in your body. Now, remember, it's indolent, which means it's sleeping. It can come back at any time, for any reason, but there are no traces of it being active." How can you ever know how you will react when you hear news like that? I hadn't actually prepared for that moment. It left me speechless, but in that exact moment, I felt like I could fly and the sky opened up.

It became very clear to me that I'm meant to be here, and I felt a creative surge of something. A jewelry line came into focus. I was thinking into the future. I saw new things and began to plan.

I could create again.

What a gift I got that day. I got my life back.

Dr. Fisher told me, even though he didn't need to, that I needed to keep doing all the things that worked to get me to that point. That would be easy to do, I assured him. Healing was deeply ingrained into my daily routine.

As Mom and I left, we were strangely quiet. I was buzzing with all the joy that came with knowing that I was fully alive, fully capable of making anything happen. I also knew that on that blessed day in May, my mom knew that her daughter was going to be okay.

Okay. I never fully understood the deep comfort of that word until I lived through a long period of time when everything definitely wasn't okay.

When I got home, all Bob could do was hug me — practically to death, it was so tight. He just smiled and smiled at me. The relief was palpable. Everyone could breathe a little bit easier. Everyone felt lighter. My mom, my husband, my kids — we could all go back to having normal relationships. I could finally answer the question "Are you okay?" with "Yes, I'm okay."

I waited to tell Frank and Summer, who had provided my acupuncture and herbs, the good news until I could do it in person. The day I told them, I walked into the clinic and chatted with the girls at the front desk. I wanted everyone, including Frank, to be there when I told them. When Frank came out of the treatment rooms, I looked at them all and simply said, "Thank you for helping to save my life and for opening up a whole new world that I never knew existed." I could never express how deeply indebted I was to them, to Alice, to everyone who had helped me along in my journey of healing. When I told them the news, everyone's eyes welled up. We hugged each other, nothing more. It was a moment of quiet triumph.

The Never-Ending Journey Epilogue

My journey of healing isn't over. It may never be in this lifetime. I still go in for a six-month checkup, but I have a doctor where I live who can do the tests and whom I trust. I go back to Dana Farber every year. I'll probably do that for a very, very long time. I'll always have to maintain where I am in relation to my cancer. It is indolent—sleeping, as Dr. Fisher says, but this Sleeping Ugly doesn't have a prince charming, and I definitely don't want this monster to wake up. The constant checkups remind me to stay the course.

I wish I could say, "I don't have cancer anymore." But in the end, there isn't a total payoff to this story. I don't want to fool myself with something that isn't fully true. I still don't show any traces of cancer in my body. I live as normal a life as can be. Yes, I'm diligent about what I eat, and I still do acupuncture and Reiki. I've gone back to teaching Pilates every day at my studio, and my clients are wonderfully inspiring to me. I make an effort to put into practice what that old bumper sticker says: "Practice random kindness and senseless acts of beauty," for no other reason than to make someone's day a bit brighter. My own world stays open and fresh. My "old" husband groans at the thought of having grandchildren, not because it will make him feel even older, but because he knows that I'm going to lavish everything I can on them.

I remember every day what I wished for when I was sick — to laugh and love, to enjoy every moment of every day — and I make sure my wishes come true with regular frequency.

I want to make something very clear. I firmly believe you can't just cut the cancer out of you, do some chemo or radiation, and think you're done. You have to cut the cancer out of your mind. You have to live, eat, and breathe positive intention. You have to find a way to forgive so that the healing can begin. You need to search every day to find serenity. And you need to make sure that you're throwing every healing modality — Western, Eastern, and lots of prayers — that you can at the disease in your body.

When Dr. Fisher told me in May of 2009 that I was a one per-center, it was a moment of triumph. Looking back, though, it was just one in many moments of small successes that added up. There is no panacea for this sort of thing — for most any disease. It took a diligent effort and a boatload of intention to beat it. We all have that within us, and know that if you're reading this and you need some inspiration on your own journey of healing, you can find it in yourself to somehow, some way, be a one percenter too.

Create Energy
CHAPTER 8

Laurie's Treasure Chest of Healing

Throughout this book, I've talked about the various methods I used to heal. I want to put them all in a chapter for you to reference in your own healing journey. Whether you have a debilitating condition like cancer or just want to live a healthier life, I hope these tips and tools for good health will give you as much inspiration as they've given me.

These tips and tools are not meant to be prescriptive. I'm not a doctor, nor do I profess to be, and if you do have any kind of disease, seek medical care—both Western and alternative. I've found the combination to be most effective, and I hope you do too.

I'm also breaking this into two parts. The first is what I call "external" techniques. These are things like herbs and acupuncture. They are those elements of healing that handle the body. The second part is labeled "internal," those things I found helpful in healing my spirit. *Integration* means to put two or more things together in harmony. I believe good health requires integration at all levels—that entails mind-body-spirit as well as Western medicine and alternative healing modalities.

And integration requires balance. I believe that only you can find that balance within yourself. It requires that you learn to listen to your body and to let go of preconceived ideas of what is right and wrong. Above all, true integration requires you to believe in its workability. I've seen miracles happen with integrating all of what I've talked about — not just in my own life but in others as well. I've also witnessed people who tried alternative approaches lose their lives. Who knows if anything would have worked; their cancer was acute. But at least they tried, and because of their efforts, they may have prolonged their life in a way that allowed them to live a productive life full of love and happiness until they were called home.

In the end, living is what this is all about. I want you to live a healthy, happy, fulfilled life free from anger and resentment. I want you to find what you want to live for and go for it with gusto. I wish you a life filled with love. So as you read this, remember to breathe and to take a break and go for a walk. Relish the feeling of being able to feel the air on your skin, the smell of the earth in your nose, the sound of the birds singing. Live as much as you can and as fully as you can — that's, truly, my wish for you.

Part One: External Methods to Heal

Chinese Medicine

Acupuncture

The backbone of my alternative healing methods is based in Chinese medicine. Half of the foundation of Chinese medicine lies in acupuncture, the other half in herbs. I could write for days on Chinese medicine, because it is so far removed from our Western views. It involves processes no one could ever imagine — that is, until you experience them.

Acupuncture is one of the most fascinating healing modalities out there. Who could ever imagine that sticking needles all over the body could help the healing process? In traditional Chinese medicine, we're talking needles from the top of your head all the way down to your toes. I understand why the average Joe wouldn't opt to have this done on a regular basis, let alone pay for it. Many of us avoid going to the doctor; and when we do, we hope there are no needles involved. Acupuncture is about as different from a shot as you can imagine, so instead of being freaked out about the fact that there are needles throughout your body, imagine each and every needle having a purpose. It allows the flow of healing energy through the needles and into your body. That's what I did, and look where it got me.

The Chinese discovered the art of acupuncture thousands of years ago and have developed it into a highly accurate science. Acupuncture works on the principle of balancing the energy of the body. Much of the history of acupuncture was lost when Chiang Kai-shek took over China in 1918, yet there are many forms of acupuncture now available. I did a form that is the standard form of acupuncture in China called TCM, which stands for Traditional Chinese Medicine. A movement started in France uses methods that are older than TCM but are based on the same principles. It doesn't use as many needles as TCM, and instead of stainless-steel needles, it uses gold and silver needles. Those who have used it find it very effective.

Then there's Japanese acupuncture and also acupuncture that uses something called an Estim, where clamps are placed on the needles and very faint electrical pulses are transmitted through to the body. Whatever the case, anyone who does acupuncture should be highly trained in TCM. Also, depending on the type of acupuncture, the needles are inserted at various depths, and while it can hurt sometimes, most of the time it doesn't—just a little prick as it goes in. What's even better is you're lying down, and you can't see the needle go in. That prevents a ton of the drama.

After my first acupuncture session, I was a little weirded out about the needles, but Mom had said to do it, and everything else about it felt right, so I kept it up. I'm very glad I did, because I have since learned of others who had cancer, went the Chinese alternative route, but just did the herbs—and didn't do as well. They either regressed or their bodies couldn't handle the herbs alone. I also know others who do acupuncture regularly, which causes the herbs and other supplements they take to work far more effectively. So I do highly recommend that you do both—acupuncture and herbs.

Perhaps they work so well in combination because of what acupuncture does. Acupuncture is the insertion of needles into the skin at specific points in order to affect the flow of energy, or Qi (pronounced chee)—the energy that gives us the ability to move, think, feel, and work. In Chinese medicine, Qi is one of the body's main constituents. It circulates along a system of conduits—meridians or channels—that correspond to the organs in the body (the liver, gallbladder, spleen, kidneys, etc.). When the flow of chi becomes unbalanced through physical or environmental insults, illness may occur. The acupuncture redirects the flow of Qi, balancing it out so that the body can heal itself.

It's a complex science, and I'm not going to try to explain it here. There's obviously a ton of knowledge about acupuncture, and I'm not a trained practitioner, so I don't even know a fraction of it. What I do know is that I definitely felt it changing things in my body, and after a while, I started feeling good. And that is the test. No matter what form you use, you should notice, if not a marked improvement, then definitely a change in your body after just a few treatments.

Chinese Herbs

Herbal medicine is rapidly gaining acceptance in the United States. When you get a cold, you may often hear people tell you to take echinacea. If it's a good, strong tincture and if you take enough of it, it will nip that cold in the bud earlier rather than later. There are a ton of Western herbs available now in health-food stores, and people are turning more and more to herbs to help them heal their bodies. Chinese herbs are a bit different from Western herbs. Western herbs work to treat symptoms. Chinese herbs, like acupuncture, work to balance Qi.

Chinese herbal medicine works because, like acupuncture, it treats energy imbalances and illness. Herbs used in Chinese medicine are derived from plant, animal, or mineral substances. Most are root-based or powdered formulas turned into liquid form, like the tea I talked about throughout the book. Patients are given a certain formula for their condition and typically drink thirty ounces a day, just like I did.

Again, these formulas can be quite bitter or taste really bad. The only remedy I ever heard anyone say "This doesn't taste so bad" about was a formula to help support the adrenals. *Everyone* else will tell you how horrible the tea tastes. Most people, including my mother-in-law, quit drinking the formula because it tasted so horrible—and things didn't turn out so well for her. So, in deference to my mother-in-law and everyone else who gave up, *don't give up on the tea*. When I drank my tea, I always remembered Grannie saying, "Eat this; it's good for you." It would taste terrible, and she would say, "Hold your nose." And that always seemed to help. After a while my body started to crave the formula, and I still call it my healing tonic. The formulas can be put into a pill form, but the pills don't have the same strength as the tea, so pinch your nose and drink it down.

Here's what my Chinese herbalist, Summer, had to say about Chinese herbs:

> Chinese medicine from a TCM standpoint is centrally based around herbs. Acupuncture is amazing, and a very important part of the process, too. But I want to address the herbs. Frank, Laurie's main practitioner, turned patients away who wouldn't drink the herbs—not that he didn't want to help. He knew the patient would not get where they wanted or needed to be without them. And then he would always say, "If we don't get them now, we'll get them later." He was all too often right. I remember a lady coming in ten years after Frank had told her if she didn't fix the imbalance going on in her body, she was going to get breast cancer. Guess what she had?

A word to the wise: it's much easier to fix things when they're small, before they create a problem. I used to go behind Frank's office in a little storage room to cry sometimes. It was hard seeing some of the patients we had. Some were so sick. Some had such a hard life. Being at a clinic where people came from all over the country, even all over the world, was an amazing experience. It wasn't always easy though, but one of the things that kept me going was I knew we could help each and every one of them. And most of the time within weeks of acupuncture and herbs, I would see people get that sparkle in their eyes start to return—a sure sign they were getting their life back. It was the way they were meant to feel.

You see, traditionally, Chinese medicine came about as a preventive medicine. It would keep the body in balance and happy. Now it is mainly used in this country as a fixer, which is okay, because it can be that too. But wouldn't it be so much easier just to keep everyone healthy? So many people take vitamins and supplements, but why not have something written out and made especially for you? I see a lot of people getting upset at the Western medicine approach. Western medicine is great and definitely has its place, but I believe people are tired of the magic pill approach: as long as you take this pill, your blood pressure will be regulated or the chemical imbalance that is causing your depression will be evened out. The body must be in balance, but an antidepressant will have the exact opposite effect. Furthermore, "chemical imbalance" is something the scientists have hypothesized but never have confirmed, and I just read a study that said that sugar pills were as effective as antidepressants.

What's worse, because the special pill is treating the symptom and not the underlying cause of the disease, the symptoms come back when the person stops taking the pill. How effective is that? A lot of people don't want to be dependent on a little pill anymore. They want to fix whatever it is that is wrong with them, not temporarily. That's where Chinese medicine comes in. When used correctly, it fixes the root of the problem. It doesn't cover up the symptoms for as long as you are on it. When you fix the root, all the symptoms go away, and you don't have to worry about them coming back. Chinese medicine and Western medicine both have their advantages and disadvantages. Sometimes the disadvantage of Chinese medicine is there are some weird things (symptoms) you go through, and it's not always quick. But like I said before, it's fixing the root and not covering anything up as a band-aid.

I can't stress the importance of this enough. I had to fix the root of my health problems, and that included both the chi imbalances in my body and the emotional stuff. But I'll get to that later.

Chinese Doctors

The Chinese have been practicing herbal medicine for as long as acupuncture. Chinese herbs have been proven scientifically as well. Doctors who administer Chinese herbs have seven years of schooling and have to pass a national test. Most good doctors go further and get their PhD. This is serious stuff, and you don't want just anyone administering your herbs.

When deciding the appropriate remedy, practitioners of TCM apply the five elements and eight guiding principles, along with tongue and pulse diagnosis, to diagnose the patient. If they're not doing that—and ask if they are—you might not be getting the right tea.

Most important for me, though, was that through the experience of drinking my herbs, I learned the futility of looking for a quick fix. Who wants to soak herbs, brew for forty minutes, strain, and put away, only to face drinking the nasty stuff all day long? It's hard enough to drink eight glasses of water a day. Try drinking thirty ounces of a disgusting tea when you're not even sure what it's doing to your body. Why would anyone believe bags of twigs that smell worse than fungus-infested sneakers can be good for you?

Most people want to take a pill and be done with it—or do chemo and leave it at that. But for me, the teas helped me to understand how organic the process of healing is. (*Organic* in that there is no set time, place, or event that you can predict.) The tea becomes a natural part of your day, just as you begin your day by taking a shower, brushing your teeth, flossing, and then preparing breakfast.) It didn't take me long to look forward to soaking, brewing, and drinking my tea. It quickly started to make more sense than merely popping pills with no idea of the long-term outcome. The beauty of TCM—the acupuncture, the herbs, the system of eating—is that it's about balancing the body, creating harmony in it.

Exercise

The Chinese are about wellness. Children start drinking wellness formulas at a very young age. They're taught the benefits and the beauty of this incredible system. Americans, on the other hand, wait until they're really sick before they start a wellness program—maybe.

Diet and exercise are important factors in Chinese medicine. There are very strict but simple ways of eating that maintain good health by contributing to an optimum balance of vital life energy. The Chinese look at foods as having a yin and yang, warming and cooling, drying and moistening properties. Certain foods are better for some people than others, depending on their type and conditions. A person with a "cold damp" condition should not eat a diet of raw fruits and vegetables (which are yin), because they would further exaggerate the loss of body heat and fluid secretion. Conversely, foods that are fried, broiled, high in fat, or spicy are seen as warming (yang), because they generate heat and stimulate circulation. A person whose diagnosis is "hot dry" should avoid these foods, according to TCM. The Chinese approach to diet is to optimize digestion and increase chi, moisture, and blood flow, and to aid organ function. It can be seen as an herbal extension; in fact, the Chinese believe that diet is one of the three origins (diet, heredity, and environment) or sources of chi. This means the foods we eat directly influence the excesses and differences in our bodies.

Qigong

Along with diet, TCM encourages a form of exercise called Qigong, which is believed to optimize the flow of Qi in the body. Qigong is another amazing system that has been around for thousands of years. When I learned Qigong, it made me sit up and take notice of how we treat our bodies. Why does it take constant abuse to the body before we decide something may not be working? I've seen it over and over: years of hard-core running, aerobics, excessive weight training, and so on, leading to knee replacements, bad backs, hip problems. Finally people either give up or turn to something like Qigong and find the beauty of this system of exercise.

Qigong (also written as chi kung or chi gong) means "breath" or "energy skill." It is an internal Chinese meditative practice that uses slow, graceful movements (and sometimes breathing techniques) to promote the circulation of chi within the human body and enhance a practitioner's overall health.

Here are several reasons to do Qigong:

- to gain strength, improve health, or reverse a disease
- to gain skill working with chi to become a healer
- to become more connected with the Tao, God, True Source, or Great Spirit for a more meaningful connection with nature and the universe.

Qigong is an integration of physical postures, breathing techniques, and focused intentions. It is not a panacea, but it's certainly a highly effective health-care practice. It's recommended as an important alternative, complementary medicine.

The gentle movements can reduce stress, build stamina, increase vitality, and enhance the immune system. It additionally has been found to improve cardiovascular, circulatory, lymphatic, and digestive functions. There are many resources, such as books and videos, available to self-teach Qigong.

There are two types of Qigong practiced: internal and external. Internal Qigong is used by individuals to maintain health and vitality, because it helps regulate and harmonize the internal energy of the body. It uses certain movements and breath work or visualization to gather and circulate chi in the body. External chi is the practice of transferring the practitioner's chi to another person for healing purposes. This form is similar to other body work and modalities used in the West, like Reiki or therapeutic touch.

I want to share a form of Qigong that I practiced during the first stages of my condition. I learned about it in a book by Frank Gibson called *Age with Energy*. There are basically eight very simple moves. The actual pictures of these postures are in his book. I highly suggest this book just to have by your side.

The United States' leading health magazine, *Prevention*, in a May 1990 article titled "Tai Chi for T-cells," reported that internal exercise may actually increase the amount of T-lymphocytes in your body. T-cells are known to destroy bacteria and are the fighters of the immune system. They possibly even destroy tumor cells. Well, this is a no-brainer for me, since my whole condition was lymph, blood, and tumor related. After a twenty-minute internal exercise workout, the exercise group showed a 13 percent average increase in active T-cells over their original level.

Pleasurable Exercise

I have long been obsessed with fitness. I started working out when I was sixteen, and I did it as a way to eat — very unhealthy. I would plan what I wanted to have for food that day and then decided how much I needed to exercise. Does this not seem a little crazy? I wasn't exercising to stay healthy; I wanted to be thin. Big difference. Exercise when done to excess, as a way to be super trim, is very stressful on the body. I ran so much my knees hurt when I walked down the stairs. In my twenties, I threw out my back. Boy, was that debilitating. I had never experienced such pain until I did it again and again and again. It was the exercise, stupid. But I wasn't paying attention to that part; I just wanted to look good. After having my two boys, I couldn't get that front-cover-of-*Sports-Illustrated* look anymore, unless I wanted to have some good plastic surgery, and since you know how I feel about going under and all, that wasn't an option. So I had to find ways to exercise that would keep me healthy, not hurt my health.

Pilates and Breath Work

My back problems led me to Pilates. I heard it was a gentler approach to the body and also called a mind-body connection. Pilates was a whole new world to me and something I enjoyed. When I first started, I had to work it into my budget, so I cut corners on groceries by not buying unnecessary, expensive items. My guys definitely didn't go hungry, but I started looking and feeling better almost immediately — and the looking good helped sell my hubby on the idea of adding the extra expense.

Most importantly, Pilates helped me feel good. It took me to another level and created a sense of peace in my mind. As I studied, I found out that it works so well because of the emphasis on breath. Breath has more benefits than most drugs. Stress creates 70 percent of disease in the body, and breathing well reduces stress. Breath work energizes the body. It takes you to a deeper place in your body. It sends oxygen to your brain, creating a euphoric feeling. It also can lower blood pressure and create restful sleep. It can power you through a move, or it can calm your system down. The biggest and most important thing about breath is that it can detoxify your body. This is huge. You don't need to take any of those detoxifying potions. You are your own detoxifying center.

Breath is life! Breath is the magic wonder pill. Air is the most important nourishment that you can receive. Three minutes or longer without breathing and you can die. Let's look at what breath work can help you do: lose unwanted weight, get a good night's sleep, improve digestion, enhance your immune system, improve your mood and mental clarity, and increase your life span. Above all, it gives you energy. You can internally fire up your system with just your breath. You don't have to run six miles to get a high. You can create this with just breath work. Doesn't that make you want to stand up and take a nice deep breath?

I thought I would share a couple of techniques that might be simple for you to do:

Kundalini breath. This is for increased physical activity or energy. Start by standing with your feet hip distance apart. Raise both arms above your head as you inhale through your mouth. Exhale through your mouth as you bring your arms down to shoulder height. Inhale again as you raise the arms above the head. Repeat for three minutes.

Balancing breath. Place the thumb of your right hand over your right nostril. Breathe into your left nostril to the count of eight and hold your breath to the count of sixteen. Cover your left nostril with the index finger of your right hand. Exhale through your right nostril to the count of eight and hold your breath for a count of eight. Repeat ten times.

Belly breath. (This more than anything else calms the system, and it's the kind of breath I use when doing all the other breathing techniques.) As we age, most of us don't breathe consciously. We become shallow breathers, thus not allowing enough blood flow to circulate through our bodies. The deeper the breath, the more oxygen. The lighter the breath, the less oxygen.

I tell my clients to practice before they go to sleep. Place one hand on your chest and one below your belly button. Focus on your belly rising and falling. Take all emphasis off your chest. Imagine as you breathe that you fill your belly with oxygen and drop your belly to release all toxins. This will help set the intention for a peaceful rest. Try to take ten healthy inhalations and exhalations, focusing only on your breath.

Just these few techniques have altered many situations for me. I could never understand why I would get shortness of breath. The more anxious I got, the shorter my breath became. I started applying some of these breaths to many situations in my life. It's what helped me get over my fear of flying. When I started feeling like I couldn't breathe — and it usually happened when they announced the doors closing—I did some belly breathing, and I would immediately feel calmer. That's much nicer than the usual feeling: like I was going to have a heart attack. When I started focusing on slow, calming breaths and telling myself I was calm, I felt calm. It doesn't get any simpler than that.

I also use healing breath when I walk. I've gone in depth about my chi walking already. I still get in my sixty minutes almost every day, and every day I come home feeling energized with appreciation for such a wonderful experience. What a gift to engage with the universe and also to be taking care of your mind, body, and spirit, only allowing healthy messages and just being in the moment. It constantly reminds me to be grateful for where I am, who I am, and how I am — and that is, perhaps, the best and simplest healing technique around.

Diet

There is more and more research out about food. I wrote at length earlier about food, but I can't stress it enough. Western doctors still don't make the connection between the food we eat and the poor health we're in. Lymphoma is becoming the fifth most common cancer. I believe that's because of all the unknowns we're being exposed to, such as pesticides, toxins, hormones, EMFs. Add some *stress* to that, and if you have a weakened immune system, this can wreak havoc in your system. Let's add worry and unresolved sadness, anger, and resentment, and you are in trouble. All this can create a chemical imbalance in the body.

I did consult with several nutritionists that didn't have any magical formulas. I guess we haven't tapped into that area much. I do know that a lot of people have food sensitivities that can harm their body and even lead to things like cancer. Common food sensitivities are wheat, dairy, and eggs. Sensitivities are different from food allergies. If you're allergic to a food, like peanuts, you eat them and you have some serious reactions. Food sensitivities won't kill you — at least on the short term. But they can wreak havoc on your health. I know people who shouldn't eat gluten, but when they do, they break out in rashes, or they feel fatigued.

One woman I know had a lot of food sensitivities; when she ate something she was sensitive to, her adrenals would go haywire. They would get overtaxed and then she couldn't sleep, because she was too jacked up on adrenaline. The hardest part was she would go in and out of sensitivities. She didn't eat wheat for about five years, and now she can eat it sometimes — but if she does it too much, there's the adrenaline rush. She overtaxed her adrenals so badly that she has to be careful; otherwise she can't do anything. In other words, she'll go back into a state of high stress and chronic fatigue, and it's amazing how much of that is caused by food.

There are no over-the counter tests for food sensitivities. However, there's something called applied kinesiology, which tests weak muscles for sensitivities. There are some good practitioners out there, and then there are some not-so-good ones. A lot of chiropractors are trained in applied kinesiology techniques. Before you go to one, check a lot of references and check their credentials. You want someone who is trained and has gotten a lot of good results in the past for clients.

Food sensitivities aside, the main advice I would give anyone — because I'm not a doctor or a nutritionist — is to try to stay away from sugar and processed food. It seems like it takes about two weeks to kick the sugar habit completely. When you first stop eating it, your body will crave it, sometimes fiercely. Eat fruit, whole grains, and anything that is naturally sweet, and just keep telling yourself that this is good and healthy. Eventually you won't crave sweets so badly. Oh, and another tip. We tend to crave sugar in the middle of the afternoon because our blood sugar has dropped from lunch. Instead of a sugar snack or even chips, try eating a hardboiled egg or some turkey. The protein will satisfy the sugar craving, and it will last you through to dinner.

Also beware of hidden sugar. Sugar is added to practically everything, so it's vital to read labels. If it's got sugar in it, don't eat it. The same holds true for chemicals. If what you're about to eat has a chemical you can't pronounce, chances are it's not going to do your body any good. And watch out for sugar substitutes. There was the very real scare about saccharin twenty years ago; it was found to cause cancer. Now Splenda is the hot, new sugar substitute. Here's a story an acupuncturist told me about Splenda. If it's true, it may make you swear off Splenda and anything like it. A woman was having neurological problems, and the doctors didn't know what was going on. Finally, it got so bad they decided they needed to do brain surgery. They opened up her skull, and along the nerve sheaths was a white, slimy substance. It was the chemical residue from Splenda. Her body obviously didn't know what to do with it, so it ended up in her brain.

It takes a little bit of work to eat wholesomely. It's so easy to buy some frozen dinners and pop them in the microwave. They taste good — they're manufactured to taste good — until you cleanse your system a bit and get off sugar. Something interesting happens when you get detoxified. Foods you thought tasted great now taste like chemicals. That's a good place to be, and it keeps you to the perimeters of the grocery store. There's a whole new world of food waiting to be found, so happy shopping and *bon appetite*.

Tools for Wellness

There's a funny irony in all of this. Wellness is my mom's field of expertise. Twenty years ago, she wrote a chapter in one of the top wellness journals, and she's on the board at Harvard for mind-body-medicine. It took me getting sick to appreciate all that my mom knows about healing. Sure, I was miffed when she told me to get acupuncture, but now I'm beyond thankful. Mom used to tell me when I would go on an exercise jag, "Laurie, that's too much. You're working out too hard. It's creating free radicals in the body."

What did my mom know—besides a whole lot? I didn't listen—until I was forced to—and then things started making sense.

Wellness means being whole and in balance. It's not something you do once and you're done with it. It's a lifestyle. It involves an investment of your time and some money, but as it becomes a way of life, you might find that you're spending far less on doctor's bills because of all that you're doing.

There's also a ton of information out there about wellness. One website that I found quite informative is www.ToolsforWellness. com <http:www.ToolsforWellness.com>. What a great name! It has in it a whole new world of wellness products. Did you know you should have a filter on your showers? You would think that the water you're showering in is pure. We step out and we think we're clean. Wrong. Our water is full of chemicals—chlorine chief among them. And as mentioned earlier, your skin is the largest organ on your body, and it absorbs chemicals quite easily. Your pores open up in all that warm water, and that's how the chemicals get in. Once we dry off, the pores close up, but the chemicals are lodged in them.

And think about this: you're drinking that chemically laden water. It's so important to filter your water. You can get shower filters, sink filters, and even whole house filters. At the very least, your water should be filtered through carbon, but that doesn't get everything. The water should also be run through some type of reverse osmosis process to clean it of all contaminants. Distilled water is also a good choice, but I've heard some bad things about plastic bottles—the plastic leeches into the water—so it would be best to get your own distiller.

Another fascinating item out there is called the Q-link. Someone came up with a metal that deflects the EMFs that surround us every day in our electronic world. You wear the Q-link and it keeps the EMFs away from cell phones, microwaves, TVs, computers, hair dryers, your LCD clock radio—the list goes on and on. I also have a crystal on my computer to absorb the EMFs. And one doctor told me that up to one hour of sunshine a day in our eyeballs—no glasses or sunglasses—helps combat EMF poisoning as well.

Dr. Oz

In the course of my studies, I read about Dr. Oz, who is a renowned cardiologist in the United States. He has been on Oprah several times, has his own TV show, and has written many books on health and wellness. Here are some of the things he suggests we all try to do every day:

- Walk thirty minutes with your heart rate elevated. Work to build up to ten thousand steps a day.
- Floss and brush your teeth to control inflammation and gingivitis, which decreases the risk of heart problems.
- Drink several cups of green tea and lots of water.
- Take your pills. A good multivitamin that has B3 niacin, B5, B6, B9, B12, C, D, E, calcium, magnesium, selenium, and co-enzyme, or you can drink a herbal tonic with the same.
- Meditate for fifteen minutes. This can take the form of prayer. The key is to search for a path that gives you deeper meaning in life.
- Sleep seven to eight hours a day.
- In a notebook, write down the top ten things you're grateful for.
- Don't diet to lose weight. Instead, eat nutrient-rich, calorie-poor foods.
- Do something for someone else that you normally wouldn't do.
- Do Qigong.
- Measure your blood pressure, heart rate, and waist size.
- Do a yoga or Pilates workout for flexibility.
- Write a thank-you note to a friend.

- Shut off the news. Be grateful.
- Do something you've never done before. Memorize a passage or an affirmation.
- Do something as a family.

Here are my added suggestions:

- Send out beams of love to the universe.
- Be present and in the moment.
- Love the ones you're with, and tell them you love them.
- Smell the fresh air. Watch a flower blossom.
- Begin your morning with only happy thoughts.
- Be thankful for where you are right now.
- Honor your elders, and thank them for their wisdom.
- Nurture an animal. Animals teach us every day about unconditional love.
- Smile, even when you don't want to. Putting a smile on your face can shift the energy in your body.
- Be in awe of nature; listen to the soothing sounds of birds. We now buy CDs to do this. Sit outside and really listen.
- Listen for a new positive change. Listen especially to a loved one.
- Breathe the best breath you can. Make it start from the base of your belly and move all the way to the top of your chest. Send the breath back down to your belly. Breathe like you are a child again.
- Cook the best meal you've ever made. Put on your favorite music, light a candle, pour a glass of wine or three, and cook your heart out.
- Call your parents and thank them for having you.
- Tell your children how much you adore them.

I believe the most important of them all is this: Forgive. Forgive yourself and forgive others. The minute we let go of resentment and forgive whomever has hurt us, a whole chemical shift will occur.

Wellness is an incredible journey. Sure, we're bombarded with threats to our health, but it's not something to be scared of. Just figure out what you can do to live a life of total wellness inside and out. Come up with a plan and implement it step by step; otherwise it could get too overwhelming. Then stick to it. Your mind, body, and spirit will feel more alive, and it gets you ready to handle the internal methods of healing (and yes, I started hinting at those in the list I just gave you).

Part Two: Internal Methods of Healing

Basically I addressed the body in part one; that's the external side of things. But if you live the healthiest of lifestyles yet don't do some internal work on your soul, you're not going to be fully alive, fully well. I said in the last section that when you're doing all those good things for your body, it makes the internal stuff easier to do.

I didn't have the luxury to ignore my internal well-being. I had to tackle everything at once. So you know that if you have to do it all, you can. It obviously didn't kill me, but it did take fortitude of spirit. Remember the old saying "whatever doesn't kill you makes you stronger." That's exactly what happened to me and could happen to you too. Ready?

Handling Resentment

I truly believe that I had so much built-up resentment that those emotions played a huge part in my sickness. I don't think there was a day that went by that some ugly message didn't enter my mind. But I didn't know where those thoughts came from or what to do with them. So I would stuff them down deep inside. The problem was, my emotions would eventually come out in some other form or fashion, mostly in the form of resentment.

Resentment is feeling angry or indignant at someone or something because of a supposed wrong they did to you. If you think about it, resentment is one step away from being a victim—and that is never okay. When you harbor resentment, a major part of you closes down. You may become bitter, sarcastic, and less able to express love—especially to yourself. You put up walls of protection, and you make your life more difficult.

But this is what I've found to be true time and again: Letting go of resentment is about me taking responsibility for what I did or didn't do in the situation, and once I took responsibility for my part in whatever caused my resentment, I found that letting it go was easy. And here's one of my dark confessions: I found that letting resentment go was good mostly for me, for my own peace of mind.

I resented my mom for years. I never could understand why she could push my buttons. I resented that she divorced my dad, even though this was a much healthier situation for both. I resented that she sent me away to a boarding school because I was difficult. It was probably the best gift she could have given me. I resented that she was so busy working to support me and my brothers that it was hard for her to connect with me. I resented that if I tried to share my feelings, it became more about her. I resented that she didn't celebrate my achievements: my good marriage, the birth of my children, my graduation. I resented that she was not the grandmother I needed her to be for my children. I totally resented that my brother Erik had preferential treatment. My mother and grandmother let me know constantly that I was the difficult one, and that equated to not ever feeling good enough. I resented that I was sent to Grannie's—I loved Grannie, but I knew that she would stab me in the back if she could. I never felt safe. By the time my mom had made a name for herself, I had stuffed so much resentment into my soul that all my conversations with her were painful. Most of the time, I would end up crying.

But you know how I let that all go? As soon as I called my mom with the news of my cancer, she stepped up to the plate and became the mom I always wanted. As I did my energy work, I recognized the part I played in all of that, and all the resentment went away.

Even with Jake I have no resentment, no anger. I forgave him in so many ways because I believe he had a sickness far worse than what I had. Jake has to live with himself every day, I don't. Once I could separate from that, I felt such a relief. And it taught me something. When my hubby and I fight, and I think he's being a rotten son of a gun, I say, "I forgive you." Whatever we're fighting about doesn't matter. What does matter is that we can get over it and move back into harmony with each other.

The most interesting thing has happened because of that. It used to matter a whole hell of a lot that I was right. We like being right, us humans. Bob and I would fight for three days, and I would make myself sick trying to be right. Now, if someone is doing something intentionally wrong, I'm going to stick to my guns, but I don't have to be right just to be right. I now look at the "rightness" issue from a new perspective. How much is being right going to drain me, absorb my mind, overpower my whole being?

Once I realized how stressful being right all the time is on a person and his or her body, I just let it go. It doesn't matter to me anymore. If someone needs to make me wrong so that they can be right, I don't care. All that matters is that I know I'm doing something for the good of it. We know that we're not right all the time. And because I've been able to let go of my need to be right all the time, Bob is more able to do it also.

Chronic Stress

I'm sure it will come as no surprise to anyone that, before the big C, I was a total stress monkey. I think I thrived on the adrenaline rush it gave me, but that rush obviously took its toll.

My mother is a stress expert. That's her primary contribution to mind, body, and health practice. Knowing what I now know, I can say with certainty that stress played a major factor in my disease. In fact, the one thing I work to keep out of my life is stress, because the cancer in my body is lying dormant. It's not manifesting in any way, but the doctors say it could if I don't watch my stress levels. It's my excuse for taking my hour-long chi walk every day. Nothing reduces stress better. However, it's one thing to say, "Don't be stressed out," and another to live it.

Let's begin with the effects of stress on health. My condition, the latent lymphoma, affects the immune system. A compromised immune system makes us more vulnerable to colds and flu, fatigue and infections. In response to an infection, or an inflammatory disorder like rheumatoid arthritis, cells of the immune system produce two substances that cause inflammation: interleukin, and tumor necrosis.

I've had so many different levels of stress in my life since birth. Chronic stress grinds away at your mental health, causing emotional damage in addition to physical ailments. Long-term stress can even rewire the brain, leaving you more vulnerable to everyday pressures and less able to cope. Much of our stress and emotional suffering comes from the way we think. I'm a master of this; I can drive myself nuts in two minutes. The thoughts that cause us stress are usually negative, unrealistic, and distorted. They're knee-jerk responses that just pop out. This idea, by the way, comes from my mom's book *Relax — You May Only Have a Few Minutes Left*.

Mom also helped me recognize that there is a joy in stress, if you know what to do. Mom is an amazing woman with wisdom and wit that I have only now come to appreciate. She writes,

> I want to help you discover that stress — the very thing that creates so much trouble for you–can also be the source of enormous humor and enjoyment. Yes, you can actually use stress as an opportunity for growth, resiliency, and humor. You can learn to use humor to reframe a stressful situation and think about it in a different way.

Here is a prime example of this. I was extremely claustrophobic. To avoid an elevator, I would take the stairs — no matter how many flights I had to walk up. During my second visit to Boston, another CT scan was ordered. Well, the first time I was on the main level of the hospital, in the CT scan with clouds on the ceiling. But this one was in the basement. I was not happy about this. Then they told us how to get there, which included taking an elevator — there were no stairs, mind you. *How is this possible in a hospital?* I thought. But I took a deep breath, got in the elevator, and didn't freak out. But then I was in the basement, where there are no windows — another one of my fears. I could feel panic coming on, but I also knew I needed to have this test.

Meanwhile, I knew Mom was sensing my fear. I had learned to deal with fear by going into a different zone; my body was there, but not my mind. I don't know if it's healthy, but it's gotten me through a lot of tight situations. Anyway, Mom and I started walking down a hallway that had signs on the ceiling with horrible names that can make you think you're never getting out of here. I kept reading the signs, totally freaked out. I look at my mom and said, "I'm out of here. This is making me crazy."

Mom asked, "Which part?"

"I don't like what the signs are saying."

"Well, just stop reading the signs."

I looked at her and thought, *How simple*. It also created a shift in my thinking: I didn't need to read the signs; I just needed to get to the place for my test. Once I knew this, my body began to relax, and then I started to giggle. Pretty soon we both laughed our asses off, and this created a chemical shift in my body.

Relaxing and letting go is a very Buddhist way of being. I studied a lot of Buddhist texts during my research phase. The Buddhists teach that without illness there cannot be health. It's similar to pain and pleasure — they're two sides of the same coin, just as in theater, tragedy and comedy are always interconnected.

Stress is going to be a part of our life whether we choose to embrace it or fight it. It's a matter of how we deal with it. We all have bills to pay, deadlines, stressful jobs, constant responsibility, family, relationships — the list goes on and on. Stress is an essential part of life, so why not find the joy in it. We're all going to worry to some degree; it's just a matter of how we react to what we're afraid of.

Here are some of the myths about stress and why they're not true:

Myth 1. Stress is the same for everybody.

Stress affects us all differently. This is for sure. What may be stressful for one person is completely different for others. Perception is everything.

Myth 2. Stress is always bad for you.

This is wrong also. Stress is to life what tension is to the violin string: too little, and the music is dull and raspy; too much, and the music is shrill or the strings snap. Stress can be the kiss of death or the spice of life. It's how you manage it.

Myth 3. Stress is everywhere, so you can't do anything about it.

Not so. You can do something about it. You can change how you look at a situation. You can turn darkness into light. Or as Mom would say, take a humorous approach.

Myth 4. No symptoms, no stress, Don't be fooled. In fact, camouflaging symptoms of stress with medications may deprive people of the signals they need to reduce their stress. Certain kinds of stress require attention. Minor symptoms, such as headaches, backaches, or heartburn should not be ignored. Mind you, I've had them all.

I have learned to embrace stress. I have learned many tools that have helped me get through things I didn't want to deal with. The biggest thing is we have the power to control our minds. If a message is coming in that we don't like, we can remove it, especially before it tries to take over. This is reframing. You can shift your perspective on situations that distress you and begin to see opportunities to become optimistic, joyful, and resilient.

Above all, learning to deal with stress has taught me resiliency. I love that word. My mom dedicated her last book to me, saying, "To my daughter Laurie for her incredible courage, grace and dignity." She always lets me know I'm doing well because I'm resilient. I believe I acquired this from her.

What does being resilient mean? Through fifteen years of groundbreaking research, Karen Reivch and Andrew Shatter, psychologists and the country's preeminent resilience research team, have concluded that resilience is what determines how high people rise above what threatens to wear them down. Resilience allows us to survive in this chaotic world with elegance and grace.

Many of us become victims of old thought patterns. We allow more negative thoughts in than positive. Just watch the news for half an hour and see how you think afterward. I bet it's negative. It's much easier to maintain old behavior patterns than to try to shift and create new ones. We can't always control what happens to us, but we can control our reactions and how we think about a situation. People who practice resiliency have developed the ability to push through problems rather than allowing the circumstances to control them. They've learned that their mind can become their ally instead of their enemy, especially through tough times.

Here are some techniques to be resilient from Mom's other book, *Kick Up Your Heels Before You're too Short to Wear Them*:

> Remember that a thought can be latched onto or let go. It can't disturb you unless you let it. Think of times when you showed courage in the face of adversity. You've been the hero or heroine of your own saga many times. Who is that person who triumphs over difficulty? Resonate with your inner warrior. Perhaps when things get tough, go to that inner voice, or even deeper, and ask for guidance.
>
> Create an attitude of strength, and learn to walk purposefully, even if you don't feel that way. People pick up on your energy. They see your weakness better than you do. Stand tall and your mind will follow.
>
> Know that millions of people throughout history have endured difficult and horrific circumstances and yet survived to tell their tale. Keep certain books by your bed. I keep them all over the house. It drives my husband nuts, but that's what makes me. The old me would have put them up to satisfy his needs. I love to read books about people who have overcome adversity, people like Primo Levi, who wrote about how he survived the Holocaust in *Survival at Auschwitz*.

Getting Rid of Worry

Worry causes stress in the body. It creates a feeling of fight or flight. It sends different messages to the brain — some good, but mostly bad. With worry comes stress; they go hand in hand. The more I worried, the more uncontrolled stress I had. I worried about everything. Grannie used to tell me, "You never know." You never know what? Well, be careful while you go on walks; someone could throw you in the back seat. Or you could go out in your car and be hit by someone. You could drown at the beach if you're by yourself. Someone could slip something in your drink while you're not looking. And how about this one: you could die in the middle of the night while you are sleeping. We're all going to die one day, so why should I worry if it's in my sleep.

The lesson was ingrained, and I worried myself sick about my children. I even perfected the art of pre-worrying. Worrying that something *could* happen. I would worry about my health to a point of exhaustion. At least I don't have to worry about getting cancer anymore. Getting on planes was exhausting, because I would worry that our plane was going to crash. Car trips were exhausting, because I would worry about getting in an accident.

But what did it get me except really sick? Worse, I have come to learn that worry bankrupts the spirit. Let's talk about the adverse side effects of worrying. First, imagine chemically how damaging these crazy, constant, awful thoughts wreak havoc on the body. The minute I started the process of worry, I could feel my body become tense, and my armpits would start to sweat. I would get a shaky feeling, almost as if I were trembling or had the chills. My mind would feel scattered, my fingers would become numb, and my head would feel tight. It was absolutely paralyzing and physically exhausting, as if I had just run a marathon. This is definitely not a healthy way to live.

What are the effects of worry on the mind? A worried mind is always preoccupied with fear, for there is no end to worry. It eventually causes all types of psychological and physical disorders if left untreated by a professional. Modern medicine and psychology have found out that worry not only affects the mind, but also the body in the most profound way. What are the components of worry? Worry can manifest on three levels: physical, psychological, and spiritual. The biological component of worry is the physiological and biochemical activity of the body. The autonomic (involuntary) nervous system reacts to brain activity and causes blood pressure, pulse, heart rate, and respiratory rate to increase. On a psychological level, the brain reacts to worried thoughts. This is the result of psychological conditioning.

What is the defense against and treatment for worry? A lot of people turn to drugs like Valium, beta blockers, and antidepressants to mask their worries. But these handle only the physiological aspects of worry, and they generally cause more harm than good. Just read the side effects, and you'll know what I mean. Taking a pill for your problem isn't going to work. Remember, you have to handle the root problem to fix the symptoms.

Confronting worry involves psychological and spiritual conditioning. That's why many to turn to alternative forms of medicine, such as meditation, physical exercise, visualization, breathing, and prayer. Breathing I've already told you about; just know that when you worry, you stop breathing well.

Next step. Catch the worrying before it starts. Shift thoughts from negative to positive. When I start to feel like I'm going to get into worry mode, I start visualizing the outcomes I want for the situation. Then I get into "logical" mode. I ask myself questions: Is it probable that the event will occur? What are the chances of this plane crashing? What are the chances of Nick getting in a car accident? Are there other alternatives to the situation? Certain questions seem to slow down the worrying process. Then I work to change my thoughts: Nick is safe; Nick is a good driver; surround Nick with the white light.

And as a fix of last resort, as my girlfriend says, worry about something else. I love that. It's kind of like the "don't read the signs" advice my mom gave me. When you take your attention off what's troubling you, often it will resolve itself.

Self-Help and the Power of the Mind

I have another confession to make: I'm a self-help junkie. I have long been attracted to self-help books, almost to a fault. Whenever I would go into a book store, I seemed to be pulled in that direction. Before the cancer, my interest was in being in shape or dieting more effectively. When I got sick, I delved into the spiritual side of things. I have to say, after a while they all seem to be saying the same thing in a different way. Good self-help books are all about using the power of the mind. We think ourselves sick, just as I did, thinking something bad was going to happen. And we think ourselves well, just as I did every day through affirmations, visualizations, and other positive mind exercises.

Self-help books helped me manage my panic attacks, but they didn't cure them. My mother says that I've suffered panic attacks since I was a child. I would get upset and turn beet red. Panic comes from thinking that you don't know what to do in a situation. You work yourself into a lather about what's going to happen anyway — and that can be debilitating. I had a truly scary attack a long while back. Bob, Mom, and I were vacationing on the island of St. John. She had a free trip and asked if Bob and I wanted to join her. I was in the "not talking to mom" phase at the time, and I thought that it might help us.

St. John is one of the most beautiful islands I had ever been on. All of a sudden, I woke up in the middle of the night with my heart racing. I felt sick to my stomach, and I felt overwhelmed with fear. There was no hospital on St. John, so if something was wrong, it had better be really wrong, because they would airlift you out, which would cost a gazillion dollars. So, there I was, lying in bed. The whole house was sound asleep, with Bob once again peacefully sleeping by my side. But I was feeling like I was having a heart attack.

I finally woke Bob up and asked if I could turn on the light. In one of his very sweet moments, he said yes and then asked me what was wrong. He stayed up with me until dawn, talking to me and letting me know everything was going to be all right. By the way, he's very good at that. Next morning, I decided to share my fears with my mom. She said it sounded like some form of a panic attack. Well, she just happened to have with her a book by Wayne Dyer called *Your Erroneous Zone*, which had a whole chapter on panic attacks. This in itself was too weird. What are the chances she would have the book I needed?

Anyway, the book got me through the rest of the week, sort of. The bad news was, I felt disassociated, disconnected. I was there, but I wasn't. I was having such bizarre thoughts and just couldn't figure out why my mind had gone off-kilter. I dropped nine pounds in one week. That was the only good part. When we got back to the States, I signed up for some therapy. I'm sure this poor woman thought I was nuts. I did, for sure. I kept thinking, *Where am I going when I die?* I also didn't want to leave the house and be around people.

This took almost two years to go away. But I did something smart: I refused to go on medication and chose to work through it with behavior modification. The meds would have handled only the symptoms; they would never have fixed the problem. The therapy didn't do much good either, except it helped put things into some perspective. We figured the panic attacks had a lot to do with both my ex, Jake, and my then boyfriend, Bob. We hadn't married yet, and Bob was very controlling at the time. I felt like I was always being disciplined and that I was being treated like a child. We have come so far, Bob and I.

But the point here is that self-help books go only so far. It takes a trained practitioner or counselor, either lay or spiritual, to help you through the hard stuff. And I have since learned that if we try to do the kind of therapy on ourselves that handling all the "junk in your trunk" requires, it can be dangerous; if we could spot what needed to be fixed by ourselves, we would do it all the time.

Handling Family

My hubby wrote a book about the secrets of football, *Winning in the Fifth Quarter: How to Apply the Secrets of Football to the Game of Life*. In it he talks about "who's on your bus." We're the bus driver, he says, and we're in control of who we have on our bus. If they're good, positive, uplifting types, by all means keep them on. If they're not—if they seem hell-bent on destroying us either overtly or covertly, then we need to kick 'em off.

This is key. Surround yourself with only loving and supportive individuals who are striving to be better, not wanting to take you down to a negative place. This works well with both people on the outside and those in your family. I've had my issues, but you know something wonderful? After I got sick, my family quit bickering and became the support system I needed. My boys became model sons. Nick stopped hanging out with the wrong crowd and got his act together. Ty called me every day and gave me positive, loving support. My brothers, Erik and Jonny, were there for support whenever I needed them. Mom, well you know how that's turned out. Even Dad, the strong, silent, Clint Eastwood type, became the dad I always wanted.

And the best surprise of all was my husband. We have grown closer, and our relationship is stronger. We've been together going on almost twenty years. I can now say the vows I took have true meaning behind them. We've been together for richer or poorer and in sickness and in health. There was a period when we both weren't sure how much time I had. I learned that nobody knows. You just make it your best day ever and hope and pray for the best.

Also, do not stay in limbo. Do not stay stuck with a message that has been delivered to you. Maybe it was someone who told you that you were standoffish when in fact you love being with people. Maybe it was your doctor telling you that you have an incurable disease. If you don't want to believe them, don't. Take a difficult experience as a challenge, and allow yourself to focus on the positive.

Many cancer patients and survivors have discovered that life becomes sweeter, their troublesome relationships are healed, and they become more empathetic toward others who are struggling as well. I never had this problem; I have always had empathy. Surprisingly, many people who suffer from serious diseases or illnesses find that their gratitude barometer reaches an all-time high. I can attest to that, from the minute I wake up to the minute I go to bed. Amen.

When I was in the middle of my cancer nightmare, I heard a song by Tim McGraw, "My Next Thirty Years." I highly suggest playing it as much as you can as a daily reminder to live your best life for the next thirty years. Lord have mercy on my next thirty years plus. This song is so powerful for me; I listen to it whenever I can. I want to be around for my next thirty years, enjoying my family. It also reminds me that trying to "keep up with the Joneses," is unhealthy. I have no desire to keep up with anybody but myself. That's difficult enough. And above all, live every moment as the precious gift it is.

Forgiveness

What made my family turn around wasn't that I was sick. I truly believe it was because I forgave them. Forgiveness was the key for my healing journey.

Bill Ferguson, in his *Online Guide to Effective Living*, helped me realize how powerful forgiveness is. I strongly suggest you read the sections in that guide on "Heal Your Hurt," and "Heal the Inner Issues That Run Your life." But if you can't, here's what he recommends in a nutshell:

- First, release the resentment. I've talked at length about resentment, and Ferguson backs me up when he says, "Look under the resentment and find the hurt."
- Find the feelings of being not good enough or not worth loving that you're avoiding. Then be willing to experience them.
- Cry if you can. Once you can feel the hurt, you no longer need the resentment.
- Recognize that the person you resent has a very particular state of mind and a very particular way of seeing life. Notice that this person has a limited awareness and acts consistently with his or her limited skills and ability.
- Notice that this person is doing the very best he or she can with his or her limited ability. Notice how much this person suffers as a result of his or her limited equipment.
- Now ask yourself if you're willing to forgive this person for the damage caused.

- Remember, forgiveness is for you, not the other person. Forgiveness is a choice. Let go of your resentment, and get on with your life.

After my work with Alice, I was able to bring forgiveness into my life. I forgave my ex-husband for abandoning me with two young boys, leaving me with no resources or funds to provide for us. I forgave Mom for her not being able to be there when I needed her. I forgave Dad for not giving me what I needed emotionally. I forgave my brother Erik for being the chosen one. It was not his fault, and he deserves whatever comes his way. I forgave my children for stressing me to the max in their teen years. I forgave Grannie for all the triangulation she caused and for lying. I forgave the universe for all that was happening to me. When I had forgiven all of that, I could embrace life, move on, and start to let go. What a beautiful thing. One of my favorite sayings is "Letting go and letting God." When I forgave, I found a peace I had often longed for but never could have. It was truly healing.

Faith and Belief

I have another favorite saying: "A little faith will bring your soul to heaven, but a lot of faith will bring heaven to your soul."

Having faith works on two levels. There's the faith you can have in yourself to be able to do anything you want, be anyone you want to be, have all that you wish for. It's like the Bob Dylan lyric, "You don't need a weather man to know which way the wind blows." You don't need a psychologist to learn that having confidence in your ability to achieve something has much to do with whether you make the effort to succeed. While self-efficacy is a scientific concept tested by psychologists in various settings, it is also common sense. When you believe you can do something, you're likely to be more successful at it than when you believe you can't do it.

Faith is believing in something when common sense tells you not to. I can attest to this. I so believed that the herb tea I drank had healing powers to it. I would imagine it navigating through my body and cleaning out all the areas that weren't well. Each sip

I took, I would say, "This is my healing potion." Mom would say I was obsessed with my tea, and I would say, "Absolutely." I was on a mission, and I could feel it working in my body.

Faith is belief. Belief is any cognitive content held as true. It's the mental state in which an individual holds a proposition or premise to be true; it's the mental acceptance of a claim as truth, or the mental act, condition, or habit of placing trust or confidence in another.

Belief can be powerful, whether negative or positive. I believe that getting well was all that mattered, so I learned to let go of most control issues that would consume my mind otherwise. I used to want to be in control and in charge. The minute I started letting go of being in charge of the universe and focused on 100 percent wellness, so many things changed.

Faith has a spiritual aspect to it too. I had faith that in every moment of every situation there was and is a plan for me. *How can this be if I'm not taking charge*, I used to think. The quick answer to that is, do I have to be in charge for something to turn out right? Oops, another lesson. The more I stopped trying to be in charge, the better off I was.

When I found faith in God, I also rediscovered the power of prayer. Prayer requires faith. Prayer has become empowering for most situations. I don't just use prayer for bad, uncertain situations. I use it for being thankful no matter what and knowing that God has a plan for me. Jesus taught his disciples that when they prayed, they had what they asked for before they actually received it. My energy teacher taught me this as well. Before cancer, I would ask for something such as, "Please, God, if I do this, this, and this then will you give me such and such as a reward?" Now I thank before I receive. I thank God for any and all gifts, and I put out the thought that things will turn out for the good of all mankind. I'm constantly aware of all that I'm surrounded by and with. And I also believe that all I've learned in my exploration of self-help has roots in faith. Clearly, Jesus was teaching his disciples a form of visualization. Read this passage from the Bible with an eye to visualization:

Jesus…saith unto them, Have faith in God. For verily I say unto you. That whoever shall say unto this mountain, Be thou removed, and be thou cast into the sea; and shall not doubt in his heart but shall believe that those things which he believes shall come to pass, he shall have whatever he believes. Therefore I say unto you, What things you desire, when ye pray, believe that ye receive them, and ye shall have them. (Mark 11:22-24)

In other words, ask and you shall receive. So many of our problems would be solved if we turned to the spirit within.

It has only been in the last twenty years that modern medicine has validated and accepted meditation and visualization therapy, and I'm so glad it has. This validates all that I have come to know about healing. It goes back to the idea of integration. Prayer, Eastern medicine, Western medicine — it can all come together to create harmony and health. This integration is now at hand, for we have entered the golden age of prayer. Prayer has reentered the hospitals and clinics of the land. In the early 1990s, only three of the 125 medical schools in the United States featured courses in which spirituality was addressed. Now researchers are studying the correlation between spirituality and health. They have also discovered that individuals who follow some sort of spiritual path (it appears it doesn't matter which), live longer and have less major illness. When I read that, I started jumping up and down and whooping so hard I scared the dogs. I couldn't believe my eyes. It affirmed what I've learned on my own journey.

What have I learned? That I am a powerful spiritual being, capable of creating anything I want. Before cancer, I created bad health and bad vibes. After cancer, I work every day to create what I desire the most. To do that, I stop and listen to my inner voice. It's always talking to me. I've learned to acknowledge it, to pay attention to it. The more junk I get out of my trunk, the truer that voice becomes, because that voice is my core. It is *me*. I believe in my power, and I hope you find the way to believe in yours.

Acknowledgments

Thanks to all the incredible people that helped me on my healing journey.

Alice McCall, my wonderful energy healer, who taught me so much about forgiveness and letting go, about seeing what I needed, and about accepting whatever God's plan was for me.

Frank, my traditional Chinese medicine doctor, who encouraged me to drink the nasty tea and made me feel all was better, even when I was scared out of my mind.

Sweet Summer, for her kindness and the big smile that graced her face when she gave me my teas.

Stan, for his calming influence, who would come to my home, bring organic vegetables, and help the healing process with his weekly massages.

My dear Janet Hardy, one of my special gems, who taught me how to be calm. She is my teacher in so many ways: My Reiki master, who took the time to teach me about energy work; also my massage guru, who guided my body through myofascial release, releasing both my body and emotions.

All my loving friends, who kept me laughing and were so supportive, always maintaining a gentleness in my presence and allowing me to be however I needed to be. Thank you for never judging or criticizing and for infusing me with love and positivity.

Tricia Northcutt, I am forever thankful for your coaching and encouraging. Boy, are you tough! I have internal scars from trying to do this book. I know I would never have done this without you. Thank you not only for believing in my story but also for the endless hours you put in to make it even better.

My big sis Jude, who on the day she found out my news drove six hours to my home and cleaned out my refrigerator. I knew you were worried sick. I am so blessed that you are the big sis I always wanted and that now have you.

My brothers, all four of them — Jonny, Erik, Matt, and Josh. Jonny, for driving five hours to be with me when I got my news. Erik too.

All of my nieces and my nephew for their love and kisses.

My beautiful sons, so full of love and life. Your love fills my heart and soul. I thank God every day for you both. And my great stepchildren, Robbie and Melissa, for your ongoing infusion of love and support. You all are the best!

Mom, I'm eternally grateful for you. You stepped up to the plate and became the strength that I didn't know was possible. When I needed you the most, you were there. Thank you, Mom, for being my mom.

Dad and stepmom, Lynda, for your support. It meant so much to me. Dad, for wanting to help anyway you could, offering to stay with me if I needed chemotherapy. Just knowing that was medicine enough.

Last but not least, my sweet dogs, Buddy and Dixie, for unconditional love and devotion, never leaving my side, and loving away the many tears.

Last but not least, Dr. David Fisher, my oncologist at Dana Farber Cancer Institute.

Many blessings, Laurie

About The Author

After starting and managing a riding academy for children for fifteen years, Laurie Beck became a certified Pilates instructor in 2004. The following year she moved with her family to Santa Rosa Beach, Florida, where she opened her own Pilates studio and has continued her extensive training while helping relieve others of their chronic pains or injuries. In 2007 she studied in the Wellness coaching program and will be continuing her education in this area in 2012.

She has spent many years mentoring under her mother, Loretta LaRoche, an acclaimed speaker, author, and international stress management consultant who has poured wit and irreverent humor on her audience for over thirty years. Following in her footsteps, Laurie's desire is to share inspiration, hope, humor, and healing with others in the universe.

In 2010 she began her journey into the world of inspirational speaking and has begun to share her difficult story with other people. Her book *I Am Living to Tell* was written to encourage those who have lost hope for a future and to inspire them to persevere in the midst of adversity. Above all, she wants others to know that by incorporating the combination of mind-body-spirit, they too can learn how to help rid the cancer from their mind and body.

For more information, visit www.lauriebeck.com.

Recommended Reading

It's Not About the Bike by Lance Armstrong
Anti-Cancer: A New Way of Life by David Servan-Schreiber
Conversations with God by Neale Donald Walsh
You Can Heal Your Life by Louise Hayes
The Dalai Lama's Book of Wisdom by The Dalai Lama
Healing at the Cellular Level by Vicky Thompson
Change Your Thoughts, Change your Life by Dr. Wayne Dyer
Living in Wisdom by Dr. Wayne Dyer
Eight Weeks to Optimum Health by Andrew Weil. MD
Minding the Body, Mending the Mind by Joan Borysenko, PhD
Healing with Crystals and Gemstones by Dr. Flora Peschek-Bohmer
Energy Medicine for Women: Aligning Your Body's Energy to Boost Your Health and Vitality by Donna Eden with David Feinstein, PhD
Happiness Now! by Robert Holden, PhD
Wherever You Go, There You Are — Mindfulness Meditation in Everyday Life by John Kabot-Zinn
Getting Through What You're Going Through by Robert A. Schuller
The Path to Love by Deepak Chopra
Meditations by Sylvia Brown
Be Anxious for Nothing by Joyce Meyers

The Purpose Driven Life: What on Earth Am I Here For? by Rick Warren

The Complete Cancer Survival Guide — Everything You Must Know and Where to Go for State-of-the-Art Treatment of the 25 Most Common Forms of Cancer by Peter Teeley and Phillip Bashe

Life Is Short — Wear Your Party Pants by Loretta LaRoche (the author's mom)

Relieve Stress by Health Journeys' Breathing: The Master Key to Self-Healing, CD

PatriotLedger.com

March 27, 2006

GET A LIFE: Don't wait to focus on what really matters
LORETTA LAROCHE

I have spent many hours coaching people on how not to make life a "stress rehearsal." Our culture constantly seduces us into believing that being busy and self-absorbed and working ourselves to death ultimately is the only way to get any relief. I have always advocated discovering how to find joy in the everyday since none of us knows if we will have another day.

Life has a way of changing in an instant, and two days ago mine did. I was preparing to go to Hingham to help raise money at Notre Dame Academy when I received a phone call from my daughter. She kept telling me to sit down, that she had something to tell me. I initially thought that it was something fabulous, but her voice told me differently.

She explained that she had discovered some lumps under her arms and on her neck but had dismissed them, thinking they were related to a recent bout with the flu. They persisted and so she went to her physician, who did a blood workup and told her she had all the signs of leukemia or lymphoma, since her white cell count was way up.

I have three children, two boys and this one lovely woman whom I have struggled with since day one. We have had a very bumpy road together. There are some valid reasons and some that verge on lunacy. I have often seen it as the mirror image of my own relationship with my mother. I have made a concerted effort in recent years to not stay attached to old baggage when I am with my mother because at this point, it makes no sense. She's 95 and I'm in my 60s. How long can we exhaust that which cannot be changed?

My daughter somehow inherited similar tendencies, keeping the fires stoked with memories of things not done and expectations that went unfulfilled, instead of focusing on some of the wonderful qualities that each of us has for the taking. But all the drama floats away when we are given news that could radically change our lives.

Her first call was to me, and I am thankful that it was. This Wednesday she and her husband will be going to a hospital in Birmingham, Ala., for more blood work and a bone marrow test. I will fly to Florida the following week to help her assess the situation and find the best treatment plan.

It is ironic that I am in a field that gives me the ability to access the best medical specialists in any given field. I have reached out to my colleagues and my friends. And now, dear readers I will ask you to please e-mail me if you have any information about leukemia or know of an expert in the area.

Please put my daughter, Laurie, in your prayers, but most of all, don't let old grievances from the past become your present and your future. Let them go and live life to the fullest.

Author, humorist, PBS star and Fortune 500 trainer Loretta LaRoche lives in Plymouth. To share your pet peeves, questions or comments, write to The Humor Potential, 50 Court St., Plymouth 02360, send e-mail to inquiry@lorettalaroche.com , visit the Web site at www.stressed.com, or call toll-free 800-99-TADAH (82324).

Copyright 2006, 2009 Patriot Ledger, The (Quincy, MA), All Rights Reserved.

I am Living to Tell

loretta laroche

From: "Erik Christensen" <erik@lorettalaroche.com>
To: "Loretta LaRoche" <loretta@lorettalaroche.com>
Sent: Tuesday, March 28, 2006 10:20 AM
Subject: Fw: resources

----- Original Message -----
From: Laura_C
To: inquiry@lorettalaroche.com
Sent: Tuesday, March 28, 2006 9:07 AM
Subject: resources

Hi, My name is Laura C. I read your article in the PL last evening and wept. My 40 year old brother was diagnosed over 2 years ago. Symptoms were lumps and bumps.....After blood tests and scans he was given a diagnosis of Non Hodgekins, small cell Lymphoma.

Talk about curve balls....My brother has 3 young children. His middle child is autistic.

I am a nurse. We have a large family. So began our search for the right health care provider. With many phone calls and emails we were connected with Dr. David Fisher at the Dana Farber Cancer Institute in Boston.

You can go on line and research this physician. I promise you will be impressed. He is the top MD in the field of blood/lymph disorders. Dr. Fisher and his staff have been wonderful. Michele is the nurse practitioner in the practice. They work as a team. We have laughed and cried with this group. They have met with my brothers young teenage daughter to talk with her about the diagnosis. No matter what we leave each appointment having laughed at least twice!. (Imagine a cancer hospital where people laugh and smile).

My brother is doing well. We have been fortunate. We pray alot! We look at life differently. We have learned to appreciate things more.

I will keep you and Laurie in my thoughts and prayers. If you connect with Dr. Fisher and Michele please tell them the handsome guy from Scituate says hello.

All my best.

Laura C

Bob Beck

From: Laurie Beck [mailto:beckloves2ride@hotmail.com]
Sent: Monday, April 24, 2006 8:11 PM
To: bbeck@sales-buildersinc.com
Subject: crying

Hi Honey,
I am crying with excitement!!!!!!!!!!! I felt that I needed to find the
answer or time and that all of this did not make sense presently. I am
blessed and feel like I have a new start on life. I still have what I have
but I am going to do my best to keep it dormant. Hopefully with all my new
experiences I can use these as tools to keep my body in harmony. I do
believe that God is telling me something and I will do my best to listen and

try to change so that I can heal. I love you, I love you, I love you, and I
need to have peace and harmony in my life. I am going to change alot of
things and some things are just not as important to me anymore. I hope you
can go with it. Introducing the new Laurie!!!!!!!!!!!!!!!!!!!!!!!!!!!!!!

Laurie beck

From: bbeck@salesbuilders.com
To: Beckloves2ride@hotmail.com
Subject: crying
Date: Mon, 24 Apr 2006 22:19:35 -0500

Hooray!!!! I love you too. Remember I have been with the old Laurie for 15
years so I hope you don't change the good things, just drop some of your
fears, anxiety, hang ups etc. My other hope is that you might have got
closer to God. I know you understand some of my foundation a little better
than you did. What you would call arrogance (yes sometimes I am and so are
you) but more times than not it is my believe that God has a plan for me and
he has been sooooooooo good to me. Heck he brought me you! The look on your
face when I knew exactly what enlighten meant was priceless. Oh yes let's
not forget I have practiced my own version of visualization for years. I do
wonder at times how well you really know me.

Laurie I love you and like I have said without you my life is over. Have an
open mind to this thought process. I wasn't there today and I am sure Dr
Fisher is the it and all. I also know he told you- you heard EXACTLY want
you wanted to hear.
UAB is one of the top centers in the country and DR E is the director so he
is pretty well represent as well. Dr Fritz - I don't know, let's just say
he is another cancer Dr which is not too shabby regardless.

My thought is this: 2 Drs said you need treatment. 1 Dr said lets do nothing
and see how it goes. Those views are polar opposites. If Dr E was some
yahoo it would be one thing but he is not. So what I thing would be the
smart, prudent and responsible
Thing to do is go to Mayo, Emery or MD Andersen and get another opinion.
Let's be safe on this.

PLEASE ask Dr Fisher to do a short write up on:
1. His view on why no action now is required at this time
2. When/ if action is required what he would prescribe first
3. Second and third

If it were me I would sent this findings-opinion to DR E for comments and
take it to Mayo or MD Andersen. I want to be safe and sure. I don't want
you to get really high and excited just to crash if something from today was
not quite right.

I REALLY WANT DR FISHER TODOA SHORT WRITE UP-PLEASE PLEASE PLEASE ASK/DEMAND
THIS.

LOVE YOU

Best Regards

Bob Beck

Patient: BECK,LAURIE J MRN: 352161(DFCI)
Author: David Christopher Fisher, M.D.

Status: Signe
Visit Date:08/03/20(

Date of Visit: 08/03/2006

PROGRESS NOTE
Hematologic Malignancy Clinic

IDENTIFICATION: Ms Beck is a 43-year-old woman with a diagnosis of marginal
cell lymphoma.

INTERVAL HISTORY: Ms Beck returns to clinic for followup of her marginal
cell lymphoma. Since her last visit, she has been feeling well with no B
symptoms including fevers or chills weight loss, night sweats, changes in
energy. She has begun an Eastern Medicine Program that involves a Chinese
herb concoction and acupuncture therapy, but is taking no new medications.
She has had no medical complications since her last visit. If anything, she
states that her lymph nodes in her neck have decreased in size over the
past 3 months. This morning, she underwent a CT scan, which shows the
presence of persistent diffuse lymphadenopathy with centimeter-sized nodes
in the neck and larger lymph nodes in the axilla. There are several
perimesenteric, periaortic lymph nodes in the abdomen that measure up to 7
cm in aggregate and there are some large iliac and peri-inguinal lymph
nodes as well. Her spleen is extremely large at 25 cm craniocaudally,
extending well below the pelvic rim. Two incidental lung nodules smaller
than 1 cm in size were also noted.

ALLERGIES: Childhood allergy to penicillin. ∗

MEDICATIONS: A mix of Chinese herbs.

SOCIAL HISTORY: The patient continues to live in Florida where she is the
owner of a Pilates Studio. Married and has 2 children. Never smokes, drinks
1 to 2 glasses of wine nightly. She is here with her mother who lives in
Plymouth.

REVIEW OF SYSTEMS: Please see HPI. All other systems are negative in detail.

PHYSICAL EXAM: The patient's vital signs include a weight 57.7 kg,
temperature of 97.5, blood pressure 118/78, pulse of 82 and a respiratory
rate of 18. On general appearance, this is a well-developed, well-nourished
woman sitting comfortably in no acute distress. HEENT: Sclerae anicteric.
Pupils are equal, round and reactive to light. Extraocular movements
intact. Mucous membranes moist without oral lesions or exudate. Neck is
supple with multiple subcentimeter lymph nodes felt in the posterior
cervical chain. There is a 2-cm lymph node palpable on the right axilla and
a 1.5-cm lymph node palpable on the left axilla. Cardiac: Regular rate and
rhythm, S1 and S2 without murmurs, rubs or gallops. Chest: Clear to
auscultation bilaterally. Abdomen: Soft and nontender with spleen that
encompasses the entire left hemi-abdomen. Extremities are without cyanosis,
clubbing or edema. Neurologic: The patient is alert and oriented x 3 with
no focal neurologic deficits.

DATA REVIEW: Laboratory values reveal normal electrolytes, creatinine and
liver function tests. Her complete blood count reveals a white blood cell
count of 9000, which is down from 70,000 reported prior to her last visit.
Her hemoglobin is still low at 10.5 gm/dL giving her a hematocrit of 32.7%.
The platelets are 207,000, her MCV is 72.8. The differential on her white
count reveals 54% lymphocytes, 38% polys with 1 atypical cell and no
blasts. A serum protein electrophoresis shows a low IgA level and is

Patient: BECK,LAURIE J MRN: 352151(DFCI)
Author: David Christopher Fisher, M.D.

Status: Signe
Visit Date:08/03/20(

otherwise normal with no monoclonal spike seen on immunofixation.

Iron studies show a low serum iron of 30 with a TIBC of 408 and a ferritin of 10.

CT scan from this morning was reviewed and results are as discussed in HPI.

IMPRESSION: Ms Beck is a 43-year-old woman with a diagnosis of an indolent B-cell lymphoma consistent with a marginal zone lymphoma.

RECOMMENDATIONS: We discussed with Ms Beck that she has significant disease on CT scan, but given that she is currently asymptomatic, there is no urgency for beginning treatment at this time. Her dramatic drop in circulating lymphocytes is an example of how her disease could wax and wane. Since she had no prior imaging, we do not have a good sense of whether her disease is progressing, if at all, and therefore we will ask her to return in 3 months to do a repeat CT scan and repeat laboratory tests. Given the burden of her disease if she seems to be progressing, we will likely recommend that she undergo treatment at that time. Given her anemia and low MCV, I have asked the lab to add on iron studies which demonstrated that she is iron deficient. I would recommend a trial of oral iron to see if this improves her hematocrit. The patient was seen and the case discussed with Dr. David Fisher.

Dictated By: RAFAEL BEJAR, MD, PHD
Attending: DAVID C FISHER, MD

I saw this patient with Dr. Bejar. I have reviewed this note, and I agree with the findings and plan. Ms. Beck has evidence of moderate adenopathy, but she is asymptomatic. We will continue to follow her with close observation.

DAVID C. FISHER, MD

Phone: (617) 632-6844
Fax: (617) 632-4422
email: DCFISHER@PARTNERS.ORG

cc:
PETER D. EMANUEL, cc

/ht 199 D: 08/03/2006 12:00:00 T: 08/04/2006 07:47:49 J: 766831 I: 766254 HS:

This document has been electronically signed on 08/14/2006 06:54:39 by DAVID C. FISHER, MD.

Thank god for what it is before it happens. It acknowledges that it has occured.

Visualization (a picture is worth a thousand words.)

Feelings - feel the feelings - Cant have the feelings until after it's happened?

Faith   have

Belief & know

Knowing - Speak - act, know

★ Become what you want ✦

Holding high vibrational energy Love, laughing, singing, joyful manifest us!

2

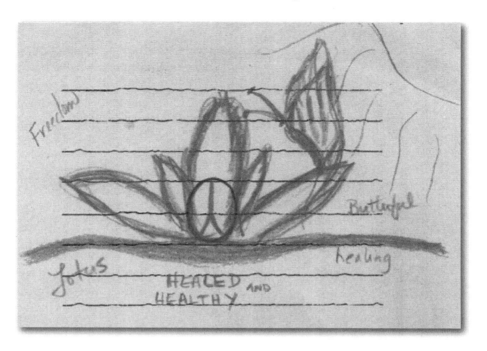

VISUALIZATION

A Picture is Worth a Thousand Words.

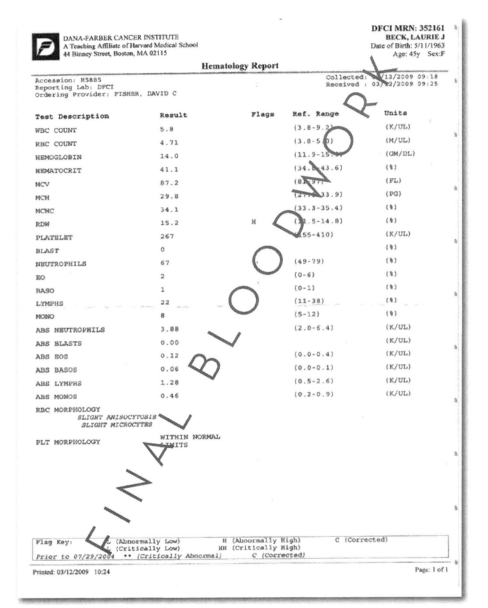

DANA-FARBER CANCER INSTITUTE
A Teaching Affiliate of Harvard Medical School
44 Binney Street, Boston, MA 02115

DFCI MRN: 352161
BECK, LAURIE J
Date of Birth: 5/11/1963
Age: 45y   Sex:F

Hematology Report

Accession: H5885
Reporting Lab: DFCI
Ordering Provider: FISHER, DAVID C

Collected: 3/12/2009 09:18
Received : 03/12/2009 09:25

Test Description	Result	Flags	Ref. Range	Units
WBC COUNT	5.8		(3.8-9.2)	(K/UL)
RBC COUNT	4.71		(3.8-5.0)	(M/UL)
HEMOGLOBIN	14.0		(11.9-15.x)	(GM/DL)
HEMATOCRIT	41.1		(34.8-43.6)	(%)
MCV	87.2		(8x-x7)	(FL)
MCH	29.8		(27.x-33.9)	(PG)
MCHC	34.1		(33.3-35.4)	(%)
RDW	15.2	H	(11.5-14.8)	(%)
PLATELET	267		(155-410)	(K/UL)
BLAST	0			(%)
NEUTROPHILS	67		(49-79)	(%)
EO	2		(0-6)	(%)
BASO	1		(0-1)	(%)
LYMPHS	22		(11-38)	(%)
MONO	8		(5-12)	(%)
ABS NEUTROPHILS	3.88		(2.0-6.4)	(K/UL)
ABS BLASTS	0.00			(K/UL)
ABS EOS	0.12		(0.0-0.4)	(K/UL)
ABS BASOS	0.06		(0.0-0.1)	(K/UL)
ABS LYMPHS	1.28		(0.5-2.6)	(K/UL)
ABS MONOS	0.46		(0.2-0.9)	(K/UL)
RBC MORPHOLOGY	SLIGHT ANISOCYTOSIS SLIGHT MICROCYTES			
PLT MORPHOLOGY	WITHIN NORMAL LIMITS			

Flag Key: L (Abnormally Low)   H (Abnormally High)   C (Corrected)
            x (Critically Low)   HH (Critically High)
Prior to 07/29/2004 ** (Critically Abnormal)   C (Corrected)

Printed: 03/12/2009 10:24

Page: 1 of 1

Testimonials

For the big book:

"The day of the diagnosis....Non-Hogkins Lymphoma and questionable Leukemia! What?? As an RN with a background in Oncology my heart sank. My dear friend Laurie had just been given the most negative unexpected news in her life. Her story is an inspirational journey how she was able to turn the worst possible situation in life to a positive, life changing experience.

Thank you Laurie for sharing your story and hopefully inspiring and helping others on their journey in life.

I love you my friend!

~ Ginny Jones, RN BSN

For the little book:

"This wise little book of healing is a gift, distilled from facing illness with courage, grace, and the willingness to be transformed by life."

~ Joan Borysenko PhD, bestselling author of "Minding the Body, Mending the Mind"

"Laurie Beck is not just an inspiration through her triumphant journey with cancer but also her love of sharing Pilates. Her passion for life is contagious. Her passion for life has changed ours!"
~ Emeril Lagasse, Chef, Restaurateur, Television Personality and Author.

"It is a privilege to be able to validate a book that encourages healing from the inside out and to feel incredible pride knowing that the author was my daughter."
~ Loretta Laroche, bestselling author of "Life is Short, Wear Your Party Pants"

"Laurie Beck is a woman with an intangible energy that infuses her passion to help people be stronger, healthier and wiser. She shares her deepest and darkest fears in her autobiography, I am Living to Tell .Throughout her narrative the reader is taken in by her open style and a message that is filled with humor and warmth.She makes one rethink old beliefs and life patterns.She not only tells us how to live but she shows us.

I have worked with Laurie for the past three years as her advisor, coach and now friend. She is a gift to all that know her loving spirit and an inspiration to those that need "a little sunshine" in their daily life.Her story is one to read and share with others."

~ Tricia Carlisle-Northcutt

Testimonials from SpaFinder.com of Laurie's studio Pilates by the Sea.

"This studio is first class in every respect. Wonderful location, state of the art equipment, but most importantly, Laurie Beck founder, owner and instructor is by far the most experienced, insightful, effective and patient Pilates coach I have ever worked with.

She is in fact a full wellness coach in my opinion. She sets this same standard for her other instructors as well. One key attribute that distinguishes Laurie and her studio is that she takes the time to deeply understand each client's unique needs, concerns, and goals. She then crafts a program to meet those needs. This Pilates studio is more than worth a trip to Florida! Don't miss it!"

~ Judy Henke, Atlanta, GA

"Only if you want to feel special! If you want to feel like the only person on earth AND get an amazing Pilates work out - you have only one choice. Laurie Beck at Pilates By The Sea. You will feel a connection with her as her passion for helping you is natural and powerful. I was never a "core workout" believer, but was curious. All I can say is that if you've never done it before or if you have - go there! Peaceful, Effective, Life Changing."

~Kristine G.

"Great studio, great people! Pilates by the Sea is a superb studio with extremely knowledgeable teachers, fun atmosphere and clean, state-of-the-art equipment. I work out there at least twice a week, if not more, and it›s always full of smiles and good vibes. It never gets old or boring as the teachers are so experienced at all sorts of different techniques, class structure and methods. They offer mat and reformer classes, as well as barre and cross-training classes. Laurie Beck, the owner, is so inspiring and enlightening. She is so full of knowledge and understanding. Tyler Beck, her son who is also an amazing teacher, is so much fun to work out with and genuinely cares about the students. I would highly recommend this studio to anyone looking to improve their body, their health or their mind and spirit."

~ Keri Atchley

"More than just a Pilates Studio. Yes this studio has all the machines, props, equipment that you would expect a Pilates studio to have. What sets it apart is Laurie Beck owner/teacher and her extraordinary approach to overall well being. I've been going to this studio for over 7 years and never get bored, am always challenged and can't wait to get back to the studio when ever I'm out of town. Laurie and her staff of teachers are highly trained, sensitive to individual clients issues and constantly continuing their training with senior teachers. From the beginner to advanced student, you will find a class the fits your level. A bonus for those that have tried Gyrotonics, Laurie is a certified instructor and has the equipment in the studio. Also try the new barre classes...another new addition to this great studio."

~ Marianne Perry

The information in this book, <u>I am Living to Tell</u>, is not intended to diagnose any physical or mental condition. It is not intended as a substitute for the advice and treatment of a licensed professional. In the event that you use the information for your own health, you are prescribing for yourself, which is your constitutional right and for which the author of this book assumes no responsibility. The author of this book is neither a legal counselor nor a health practitioner, and makes no claims in this regard.